Scandal
Essays in Islamic Heresy

SCANDAL
ESSAYS IN ISLAMIC HERESY

PETER LAMBORN WILSON

Library of Congress Cataloging in Publication Data

Wilson, Peter Lamborn.
  Scandal : essays in Islamic heresy.

  Bibliography: pp.
    1. Heresies, Islamic. 2. Islam -- Customs and practices.
3. Sufism -- History. I. Title.
BP167.5.W55   1987   297   868892
ISBN 0-936756-13-6
ISBN 0-936756-15-2 (pbk.)

Autonomedia, Inc.
55 South 11th Street
P.O. Box 110568
Brooklyn, New York 11211-0012 USA

Printed in the United States of America.

Contents

Dedicated to Elémire Zolla

1

Introduction

Arbitrary Definitions

When Mansur ibn al-Hallaj stood upon the gallows in Baghdad and died (922 AD) for the boast of *ana'l-haqq* ("I am the Real"), his martyrdom was approved not only by the hyper-orthodox anti-sufis of the city, but also by Hallaj's own fellow sufis and masters, including the great Junayd. Mullas and mystics joined to sign his arrest warrant.

The charges brought against Hallaj at various times also included a belief in the heresy of Incarnationism (*hulul*); some close association with the extreme Ismaili Qarmatians (who were later to succeed in stealing the Black Stone of the Kaaba from Mecca); and writing a defense of Satan as "the perfect sufi and perfect lover" in his *Kitab al-tawasin*.

Since Hallaj's death he has been mentioned by nearly every sufi writer. Indeed, everyone who thinks about sufism must come to terms with the story of Hallaj. Why did Junayd condemn him?

In Persian poetry, the death of Hallaj becomes a trope, almost a cliché. The gist of the metaphor is usually: "You too must die upon the gallows, like Hallaj, if you would be worthy of the Beloved." Taken at face value, this would seem to imply: "You too must embrace the heresies of Hallaj, if you would be a sufi."

But this interpretation would be as simple-minded as believing that sufis are drunkards because they write about wine. The parable of Hallaj is a great deal more complex. For the sufis the death of Hallaj is a kind of Passion Play. In this sort of theater, the martyr or sacrificial victim must always know, foretell and accept his own death as somehow inevitable and cosmically correct. Thus Jesus went to his crucifixion (or so the Christians believe); thus Husayn, grandson of the Prophet, went to his martyrdom at Karbala—although he battled to the end. In Massignon's *La Passion de . . . Hallaj,* the parallel with Jesus is made clear: the sufi martyr died to enact some truth so terrible it demanded a holocaust.

Sufis accept the doctrine of *ana'l-haqq* on some level, otherwise they would not use it as a trope in their poetry and discourse. But a sufi who is also an orthodox Moslem must also accept that Hallaj's truth cannot be openly stated without reservations, for to do so threatens the very fabric of orthodoxy. Such sayings are known as "ecstatic utterances" which shatter the bounds of language and must be interpreted, not taken literally. "I am the Real", without such qualification, is a scandal, a ripping-open of veils upon veils, a revealing of something which cannot be spoken. Even the Prophet himself mentioned certain secret moments of revelation, saying, "If the Moslems knew of them, they would stone me."

So Hallaj becomes the willing scapegoat, the ecstatic martyr—and thus his orthodoxy is restored. Hallaj must in effect consent to his own death to make sufism possible within Islam. That death then becomes a symbol of the voluntary surrender of the ego which the sufi must perform, first to his *murshed* or master, then in the Annihilation of self in the Real (*fana'*), the spiritual Death-before-death.

Afterwards, the sufi enjoys Permanence of Self in the Real (*baqa'*), just as Hallaj ascends to Paradise after his martyrdom.

However: another and different interpretation of Hallaj's death might be entertained. The hagiographic and miraculous account of the martyrdom, after all, was written well after the event, and can be accused of special pleading. The actual historical facts are shrouded in the usual mist of legend.

Hallaj is also claimed by the Ismailis. In their eyes, the doctrine of *ana'l-haqq* discloses the secret of the Imam-of-one's-own-being. These teachings are discussed at some length in Chapter Two of this book. Here it need only be pointed out that for the Ismailis, this doctrine signals the abrogation of outer Islam, the dissolving of all exoteric Law. Those who experience this truth, like Hallaj, are freed of all concealment, all the chains of duality. They reside in the *baten,* the esoteric. Sufis like Junayd have not passed along the Path for they remain within both *Shariah* and *Tariqah*. (Both these words mean literally "path" or "road", the first referring to the Path of correct action, the Divine Law; the second to the spiritual Path of sufism.) An Ismaili would say that the Junayds of this world, for all their wisdom, have yet to reach *Haqiqah*, Reality itself. Hallaj was not killed as a willing martyr to orthodoxy, but as its victim. True, the esotericist must have the courage of Hallaj and the willingness to undergo spiritual "death"; on these points

Ismailis and sufis agree. But for the Ismailis the blood of Hallaj was spilled unjustly, not as a Passion, but a tragic error.

Moslems in general believe that one should live and fight for one's faith. Passive Christian-style martyrs are relatively rare. The belief that warrior-martyrs are assured of Paradise makes Moslems willing to face death, but not to turn the other cheek. In Shiism the doctrine of Concealment (*taqiyya*) teaches that one may dissimulate one's true beliefs in order to avoid persecution. A useless death is simply waste; the purpose of life is to live and realize truth, not throw away God's gifts. Man's duty is self-perfection, not suicide. One may risk death, for risk enhances perception of the Real. But as the dervishes say, it is better to be "clever" (*rendi*) enough to drink wine in secret and not get caught.

Trying to decide whether Hallaj was a "heretic" or not is a fool's game. First, as will become clear, heresy in Islam cannot be defined with very much precision. If one sees Islam with the eyes of an orthodox sufi, then Hallaj appears to be an orthodox sufi. If one sees Islam as an Ismaili, Hallaj appears to be an Ismaili. If one sees Islam as a Wahhabi fanatic, Hallaj was certainly a heretic, and deserved to die with or without his own consent.

Whom can one believe? No Vatican Council will define terms for us. In a sense, Islam appears to be a shifting spectrum of heterodoxies, in which no absolute color of orthodoxy or heresy can be clearly discerned. One must adopt a point of view within Islam in order to make sense of the spectrum. But even then many difficulties arise unless one simply accepts the word of some single authority or master. Perhaps it would prove more valuable to make essays or forays into various heretical or heterodoxical subjects, without too many preconceived ideas or ready-made definitions. In the broadest and vaguest and most general sense however we can make up a few working definitions for use in our explorations.

Let "orthodoxy" be defined simply as mainstream Sunni Islam, the historical contours of which are clear enough, though broad in scope. This includes mainstream sufism as well, the school of Junayd and Ghazzali.

Ithna' Ashari Shiism has its own "orthodoxy" and sees itself as central and pure Islam. Nevertheless Shiites are the minority. They cannot be considered actual heretics from a Sunni point of view, because they adhere to the Five Pillars and follow the Shariah. But Shiism could fairly be called "heterodox"—and as long as the word is used loosely and colloquially, it can be applied to other Law-abiding but non-ordinary types of Islam, such as Shiite sufism or Fatimid Ismailism.

We may use the word "heresy" to describe a sect of Islam which rejects some basic Islamic principle, or the Five Pillars, or the Shariah, or claims to follow a prophet after Mohammad—yet still considers itself an Islamic sect. (For example: the Nizari Ismailis, the Bektashi sufis, the Ghulat or Extremist Shiites, the "Lawless" dervish-orders such as the Qalandars, and the puritan Ahmadiyya of Pakistan.) In using these terms, needless to say, no value judgements are implied. These are not theological or legal definitions, merely parts of a working vocabulary.

Some heresies regard themselves as no longer Islamic, even though they may have grown historically out of Islam. The Druzes of Lebanon, the Bahais of Iran, Subud and the other Kebatinan sects of Java—these might be called "schisms". In this category also we might include syncretistic sects which mix Islamic elements with other religions to produce a new religion or Path such as the Din Ilahi of the Moghul emperor Akbar or the sufi-tantrik Bauls of Bengal or the Gujerati Khojas who recognize Ali as the Tenth Avatar of Vishnu.

Finally we can adopt the term "hyper-orthodox" to

describe the bigots, fanatics, Wahhabis, Khomeiniites, sufi-killers and puritans—"donkeys in turbans" as Jalaloddin Rumi called them.

Provided we do not expect this vocabulary to function like the terms of a mathematical theorem or the technical language of Scholastic philosophy, we should be able to use it to construct a very rough map on which to place the various phenomena discussed in this book. The purpose of this exercise however is not to arrive at final definitions, but merely to provide a framework for thought.

Islam, perhaps more than any other religion, is characterized by the tension between Outer and Inner, Exoteric and Esoteric, Law and Path. In Hinduism the vocabulary we have suggested would be useless and absurd. Islamic thought deals with dialectic in a way foreign to earlier and more "primordial" faiths. The balances and conflicts between orthodoxy and heresy define to a certain extent an Islamic way of thinking about Islam. We must adopt this method, even if we do not adhere to any single point of view within Islam. Otherwise, we would be reduced to studying phenomena as rank outsiders, with no reference points to guide us, no "stars to navigate by" as the Prophet said.

We will never ask what heresy is, because to the heretic it is truth and to the orthodox it is error. Instead we will ask what heresy *does*. How does it produce its scandal? What happens when the veil is ripped asunder? What role does heresy play in Islamic culture, how does it influence art and literature?

Who cares whether Hallaj was orthodox or heretic? The interesting question is: "What did he mean by *ana'l-haqq?*" To attempt an answer, we must begin by using words with a certain purposeful gaucheness and inexactitude. Prose can rarely accomplish more than this. If by the end we have not discovered some poetic facts, we may discard words altogether and rely on other techniques of transmission.

Heresy As A Means Of Cultural Transfer

"Heresies" are often the means for transfer of ideas and art-forms from one culture to another. Persia could not have become Islamic, despite its military conquest by the Arabs, were it not for the heterodoxies of Shiism and sufism, or outright heresies such as Nizari Ismailism, Hurufism and the Ghulat. Northern India could not have been Islamicized without sufism—which ranged from the impeccable orthodoxy of the major orders to the "Lawless" Qalandars, the speculations of Dara Shikoh and Akbar, and popular syncretisms such as the Husayni Brahmins of Kashmir, the Khojas of Gujerat and Bombay, or the Bauls of Bengal.

In India in 1970 I met a woman who typified for me the kind of mystical cosmopolitanism possible only to one of dubious orthodoxy. Raihana Ben was then quite aged, and has since died. Born a Moslem, she became interested in sufism under the influence of Mahatma Ghandi, and after his death she settled near his monument in Delhi. She expressed her teaching in purely Hindu terms, and wrote a book called *Heart of a Gopi* in which she represented herself as one of Krishna's love-stricken cow-herding maidens. She believed in the complete compatibility of Islam and Hinduism.

Since the Moghul period sufism and Vaishnavite Bakhti Yoga have influenced each other in Northern India. Islamic and Hindu art and spirituality produced a civilization of tolerance, creativity and beauty. The colonial period almost destroyed this world, and the communal hatreds aroused by Partition have made it seem even more remote. To meet Raihana Ben was to meet the whole history of Moslem-Hindu love and mutual understanding from Akbar to Ghandi, and to realize that hatred can be overcome by spiritual insight. She was a bridge between two cultures.

Medieval Europe might have absorbed much less

Islamic/Greek/Oriental culture from Spain and elsewhere were it not for scholars of dubious orthodoxy such as Raimundo Lull, Roger Bacon, the alchemists and Ceremonial Magicians, the Kabalists and Renaissance Neoplatonists like Pico, Bruno, the Fideli d'Amore.

In this cultural role heresies are like fortuitous or even deliberate mistranslations of texts. To draw an analogy: a translation of Plotinus' *Enneads* was made into Arabic and Persian under the title "Aristotle's Theology". Thus Greek philosophy in Islam came to be seen in a much more Neo-platonic light than in the West. For Moslems, both Plato (Aflatun) and Aristotle were "prophets" and clearly mystics—and the entire Ishraqi School of Islamic metaphysics owes much to this fortuitous misunderstanding.

Moreover, Suhrawardi of Aleppo, founder of the Ishraqi (or "Luminationist") School of philosophy, was executed for heresy (by order of Saladdin, in 1191). By no means do all Moslems consider him to have been a genuine heretic. But the fact of his martyrdom points to a connection between heresy and cultural borrowing, for Suhrawardi attracted the rage of the hyper-orthodox by his adherence to Greek and ancient Persian ideas.

Since every translation is in part a mistranslation, it might be claimed that all cultural transfer depends—to that precise degree—on such deliberate or fortuitous transmutations. Doctrinally the Koran *cannot* be translated. All versions in languages other than Arabic are at best maps of a country that must be visited in person. However, scripture never stands by itself (except theoretically in "puritanism"). Hermeneutics and exegesis must be carried out if a scripture is to extend its influence beyond the homeland and first generation of a religion— even by "puritans". As for the Bible, which doctrinally can and must be translated, certain transmutations of single words have led to major schisms in Christianity, and to a sectarianism that spread Christian teaching and culture to nations that might otherwise have resisted it (Pelagianism in Europe, Iconodulia in near Asia, Nestorianism in far Asia, Monophytism in Africa, etc.).

In Shiism many Koranic verses are hermeneutically explained as referring to the primacy of Ali and the Household of the Prophet. This exegesis emerges from the very heart of Shiism; and it exemplifies the reasons why Sunnis consider Shiites to be heterodoxical if not heretical (and vice-versa). Historically the Persians felt allied to the Alid cause because Husayn, Ali's son, married into the Persian royal house, and also because Salman al-Farsi—the Persian Companion of the Prophet—was adopted into the Household and fought for Ali. Shiism appealed to Persian royalist and legitimist sentiment, and also allowed for freer theological and philosophical speculation than Sunnism. If Islam had not been "translated" to a certain extent into Shiism, and into sufism, and eventually into various "languages" even less orthodox, the Persian majority might well have remained Zoroastrian. (Today in fact Zoroastrian mystics quote sufi poets—such as Hafez and Hatef of Isfahan—to explain their own tenets. Thus even the non-converts to Islam are "islamicized" to a certain extent.)

Because the basic structure of Islam is simple and "democratized" in the sense that "every Moslem is his or her own priest," it has proven highly adaptable to various cultures, perhaps more so than any other World Faith. Indians and Africans could not accept a religion without music, and there exists no Pope of Islam and no doctrinal authority powerful enough or even interested enough to consistantly prevent sufis from teaching Islam through songs or drumming. Outbursts of hyper-orthodoxy do of course occur. Militant Islam-of-the-sword has always existed and always will. But hyper-orthodoxy cannot define or de-limit Islam. The Prophet himself said that whoever greets you with "salaam aliekum" must be considered a Moslem. Tolerance and intolerance are both integral if paradoxical parts of Islam. Cairo under the

Fatimids, Delhi under Akbar, Moorish Granada: these must be set against the Khomeinis and Wahhabis if we are to see the whole of Islam and not merely the latest or most vivid example of bigotry and cultural reaction.

Because Islam lacks dogma in the Christian sense, it frequently proves utterly impossible to label a movement unequivocally heretical or heterodox. Some pious practising Moslems accept even Ismailis as within the bounds of orthodoxy, even though the Ismailis have abandoned the five daily prayers. The Ahmadiyya of Pakistan, however, who are fanatically "orthopractic" and puritan, are rejected even by the most tolerant sufis. Why? Because the Ahmadiyya regard their founder as a prophet *after* Mohammad, while the Ismailis accept no new Revelation after the Koran. The Bahais are severely hated in Iran for similar reasons. As for the Ismailis, they too have suffered endless persecution and rejection despite their claim to be Moslems. Ghazzali condemned them. Even Guénonian-Traditionalist sufis, who believe in the transcendent unity of religions, spurn the Ismailis as heretics.

The definition of heresy depends on whose interpretation, whose hermeneutic one accepts. No Moslem is forced to accept anyone's dicta on the subject—at least in theory. (In theory all Christians are pacifists. So much for theory.) In practise, like every other organized religion and indeed like most human institutions, Islam offers a dreary record of prejudice, xenophobia, unjust war, slaving, and suppression of dissidence.

Ideally, the consensus-of-the-community (*ijma'*) should play the role in Islam which only the Church hierarchy can play in Catholicism: the final authority on interpretation of doctrine. In practise, sometimes secular rulers usurp the role of the community, and instead of defending the Faith, try to define it. Sometimes the doctors of the Law, the *ulema,* usurp the role as they have in today's Iran. Taken as a whole, however, Islam is probably more latitudinarian than Christianity—if only because Islamic doctrine is not so rigidly defined. Moreover, Islam considers itself as much a way of life as a religion. Provided a Moslem follows this way of life, his personal relation with the idea of the Divine is largely his own affair. As a result, tendencies which might well be called heterodox often move more easily through Islamic culture than through Catholic culture.

Observe for example the difference between Islam's view of other religions and Christianity's view. Even for Dante, "enlightened" as he may have been, the Wise Pagans were denied Paradise. But Mohammad speaks of 124,000 prophets who preceded him among every nation, and he taught friendship and tolerance for the People of the Book. Jalaloddin Rumi, among other sufis, accepted disciples of different religions—something no Christian saint has ever done.

Islam and its culture exist in two modes: the crystalline and rigid, as well as the fluid and arabesque. In the former mode it remains static, "perfected" and impervious to outside influence. In the latter mode it has served to absorb and transfer huge amounts of non-Islamic cultural material, ranging from Greek medicine and philosophy to Indonesian shamanic drumming (which until recently was employed instead of the *azan* to call the faithful to prayer in the dense jungle of Java.) One cannot say that all non-Islamic material is heretical or heterodox, nor can one say that all of it can be and has been successfully absorbed by pure orthodox Islam. Some of it can be absorbed only when culture itself undergoes a transmutation, a change that may appear as heresy to the pious.

Oral Transmission

In the study of these matters, oral history can be more enlightening than many written sources. Persian esotericists have a saying: "The pen is in the hand of the enemy." Gnostic sects vanish without trace except in the published fulminations of some heresographer. Mystics who are likely to be persecuted for their beliefs keep few written records, and often these are destroyed or lost. The Shiite concept of *taqiyya,* "permissable dissimulation" or Concealment of one's true beliefs to escape oppression, has led to much misunderstanding and obfuscation. In "folk" religions such as the Kurdish Ahl-i Haqq, the illiteracy of most devotees leaves oral tradition as the only source for certain information.

Therefore, rather than speculate about vanished sects of the past or those with which I have had no contact, I prefer to pass on first-hand information whenever possible, even when I can offer no scholarly proof for my assertions. The Qarmatians who stole the Black Stone of the Kaaba, the Zinjarite slave rebellion, the role of Shiite extremists in the rise of the Safavid dynasty of Iran, shamanic influences on the Bektashi Order of Turkey, the Manichaean-Buddhist-tantrik sources of the Ismaili *Umm al-kitab* (*Matrix Book*): these matters might be elucidated by scholarship—but anyone who follows the clues in the Bibliography of this book can undertake such research.

Most of these essays arise out of a mixture of reading and oral transmission, but I have not always indicated whether my source for a given assertion is a written text or a spoken word. Sometimes good manners (*adab*) forbid mentioning a name, but aside from that I have followed to a certain extent the mode employed by Islamic esotericists themselves, who consider books misleading without some "heart-to-heart" explication. Traditional Islamic texts frequently quote without attribution, prefacing a remark with, "One of the shaykhs says. . ." or something of the sort. On occasion I have done the same when quoting an oral source or—to be honest—a phrase or verse I once heard somewhere but cannot recall where, when or from whom.

Sometimes oral sources in mysticism fail to throw very much light on real history, "true facts". Oriental mystics do not feel the same concern for such trivia as we Westerners. For example: for some time in Iran I heard and read about the Kakhsari ("Dusthead") Order of sufis. The last few colorful wandering dervishes in patched cloaks to be seen in Iran usually belong to this order. According to the Russian scholar V. Ivanov the Kakhsari *silsila* or "Chain of Transmission" from shaykh to shaykh is an historical impossibility, including people who could never have met and expanded with the names of favorite sufi poets such as Hafez and Baba Taher. Ivanov claimed that the higher-ranking Kakhsari dervishes were inducted into the heretical Kurdish sect of the Ahl-i Haqq, the People of Truth. I also heard it said that the Order began as a "secret service" under the Safavid shahs, who were themselves sufi masters. I also heard it said that the Order had branches in India.

When I finally obtained a chance to meet a Kakhsari leader, Shaykh Anvar of Shiraz, I asked him about all these points. When I was finished he smiled and said, "That's not important; you can find all that in books. What is important is Love." And for the next hour he talked about Love, and quoted from Hafez. The Shaykh presided over a beautiful garden in Shiraz, not far from the tomb of Hafez; it is called the Bagh-i Chehltan, or Garden of the Forty Bodies, because of the forty anonymous tombs it contains. No one knows who is buried there. All is legend, all is roses and cypresses and poetry. The lights were turned out, the dervishes sang and wept.

The information I wanted is *not* available in books, so most of my questions remain unanswered still. As I left the garden, I did notice some photographs of Kurdish Ahl-i Haqq *pirs* (leaders) tacked to a wall, so I assume there does exist a connection between the two groups. The only thing I learned for certain is that Love is more important than scholarship, and I treasure the rebuke I received from Shaykh Anvar.

Nevertheless, the Westerner's mind is curious and needs to be fed with some facts, lest it starve in misery.

❖   ❖   ❖

In *Bidar, Its History and Monuments* by G. Yazdani there appears an old photograph taken at a sufi shrine in South India. Dervishes of the Nematollahi Order have congregated with Hindu saddhus of the Lingayat sect, sometimes called Phallus Worshippers. (For beautiful translations of their hymns, see *Songs of Shiva,* listed in the Bibliography.) Perhaps this festival is still performed, but without actually attending it how can one be sure exactly what the photograph means? The photograph is a "fact," but without some exegesis it remains indecipherable.

The Nematollahi Order originated in fifteenth century Persia as a Sunni confraternity. In the sixteenth and seventeenth centuries it played a role in the renaissance of extremist Shiism which resulted in the conquest of Iran by the Safavi Order (an army of dervishes led by a fourteen-year-old boy, Shah Ismail) and the establishment of Shiism as the state religion.

A Moslem king of the Deccan in South India invited shaykhs of the Nematollahiyya to the Subcontinent, and the Order established itself around Hyderabad—without ever extending its influence much beyond the Deccan. The Indian branch became Shiite as well.

In the eighteenth and nineteenth centuries the Order experienced a tremendous burst of popularity in Iran again. A number of masters and dervishes were executed for heresy by the ulema. One mystic named Mushtaq Ali Shah, who is said to have outraged the pious citizens of Kerman by playing the call to prayer on his sehtar, was publicly stoned to death. (I once talked with a man who knew a man whose grandfather, as a boy, had been present at that occasion.)

What scandalized the mullas and drove them to such bitter persecution? The dervishes dressed in their own special costumes, they wandered about from town to town, they owned nothing and sometimes begged for a living, they played music and danced. By their own reckoning the sufis were orthodox Shiites, and probably most of them followed the basic precepts of the Shariah. In their own eyes, indeed, the Path they followed was pure and genuine Islam. Many tolerant Moslems, with a traditional respect for sufism, accepted these dervishes as holy men. Why then were they killed?

The collapse of the Safavid dynasty led to a split between the Shiite ulema and the sufis. Both groups had helped the Safavids to power. But the mullas declared that true initiation can come only from the Hidden Imam and that sufi masters had usurped this role. This is far from being an obscure theological quibble. At root, the quarrel concerned the vital question of spiritual authority—which in Islam can and ought to mean political authority as well.

Under the Safavids—in theory—throne, sufis and ulema were united in a single sacred kingdom. Shah Ismail claimed to speak for the Hidden Imam, and the ulema accepted this—at least in public. In private however the three parties began to struggle for precedence even before Ismail's death. Sufism lost power by this dabbling in politics, but the ulema gradually increased their presence till the last Safavid shah was no more than a mouthpiece for their decisions. After the fall of the Safavids all three parties were thrown into a new struggle.

The Nematollahi "madmen" attracted hundreds of thousands of devotees in an atmosphere of enthusiasm and revival. Among them were high-ranking courtiers of the newly-founded Qajar dynasty. This upstart Turkoman tribe desired some authentic spiritual validation of its supremacy. The mullas denied the new dynasty any mandate, so the Qajars sought out sufism in imitation of the

Safavid theocrats. At one time the shah himself, Mohammad Qajar, his prime minister and most of the vazirate
were practising sufis, and held sessions of music and
invocation in the throne room.

The persecution of the dervishes must be seen in the
light of a struggle for control of Shiite Persia between the
ulema and the emperors. The Qajars proved unable to
protect the rank-and-file dervishes from the wrath of the
mullas. The Constitution of 1906 was clergy-inspired.
Under the Pahlavis the battle went on, and was finally
won in 1978 by the clergy and the Islamic Republican
Party—who have renewed their persecution of the sufis
along with other minorities.

In their attacks on the Nematollahiyya, the hyper-
orthodox of nineteenth-century Persia could point to
several instances of heresy or association with heretics.
For example the Order numbered among its members
several aristocratic Ismailis, both in Kerman and at Court in
Tehran. The first Aga Khan himself was initiated into the
royal branch of the Order.

Later the Aga Khan raised a rebellion against the
shah. When it failed he fled to India. But he kept in
contact with the sufis. He and his successor, the second
Aga Khan, continued to send gifts to Nematollahi masters
in Iran. Ismailis travelled from India to Iran and sufis
visited Bombay to initiate Ismailis.

Finally when the third Aga Khan visited Tehran the
relationship foundered. He expected the current Nematollahi
master to visit him, and the master expected the Aga
Khan to visit him. Over this question of protocol the two
Paths parted ways. Writers on both sides now tried to
denigrate each other and minimize past contacts. Some
Ismaili texts (in Gujerati) are actually full of outright lies.

By the time I tried to investigate the story, very few
Persian sufis still remembered any details—but enough
oral sources remained in the 1970's to clear up the confusion caused by the quarrel.

From the point of view of Islamic Jurisprudence, the mullas were correct to question the entire relationship. Ismailis are clearly outside the Shariah and therefore heretics. No orthodox Shiite should have accepted such "blameworthy ones" as disciples without demanding that they first abandon Ismailism.

However, the relationship is also "illogical" from the Ismaili point of view as well. If the Aga Khan is the Imam of Shiism, the perfect master and rightful source of all spiritual authority, then why should he or his followers seek instruction from mere sufis?

Sufism claims to be older than Islam. Sufism is not a religion, and ultimately exists above and beyond all labels and categories. Most sufis are practising Moslems, true, and most will not accept non-Moslem disciples. Some do however—like Rumi, or Lal Husayn Qalandar of Lahore. Ultimately sufism claims a certain independence, not perhaps from "Tradition," but from the constraints of exotericism.

So the explanation of the Ismaili-Nematollahi connection must be sought in terms appropriate to pure esotericism. When a powerful spiritual master arises in the East, he will attrtact disciples of all faiths. The sufi poet of Benares, Kabir the Weaver, found no Moslem master fit to initiate him and so tricked a Hindu guru into doing it. Categories of orthodoxy and heresy are ultimately of no interest compared with the supreme value of realization. The Ismailis who "fell in love" with the musician-martyr Mushtaq Ali Shah could spare no thought for missionary piety. Love for them seemed a matter of life and death, not of laws and precedents.

The story behind the photograph of the Lingayat "Phallus Worshippers" and Moslem dervishes must have begun in a similar manner. By the time the camera recorded it, the relation may have become empty ritual, a ceremony of mere tolerance and devotion to some vague mystical sentiment. India is an archaeological repository of such rituals. But somewhere, sometime, some dervish and some saddhu locked eyes in an accidental glance in a moment of pure intuition and grace. The spark they lit burned away all dualities. For as Mahmud Shabestari said, "If the Moslem only knew what Islam really means, he would become an idol-worshipper." Where beauty and inspiration are found the seeker turns toward them, in whatever guise they manifest themselves.

❖   ❖   ❖

Java was converted to Islam by nine semi-legendary sufi "Walis" or saints. Most Javanese are Moslems now, but a great many of them do not practise the Shariah and are called "nominal Moslems." In reaction to this laxity a reform movement was born in the nineteenth century, inspired by Wahhabi and proto-Pakistani modernist-puritanism.

The nominal Moslems preserve Javanese tradition, but the reformers attack it and attempt to substitute "pure Islamic values." But syncretism is too deeply rooted in Java to be easily eradicated. In truth, most Javanese follow a religion that can only be called "Javanism," which owes as much to shamanism, Buddhism and Hinduism as it does to Islam.

For example the Moslem Sultans of Solo (or Suryakarta) in East Java boasted a special "marriage" with the green goddess of the sea, Loro Kidul. Once a year the king would retire to a tower and summon up the goddess for a night of intercourse. His continued power depended on her patronage. Loro Kidul is a dangerous deity; no one swims in the sea near her shrines lest they fall into trance and be washed away to drown. Such royal magic is risky business, and recent Sultans have abandoned the practice.

Indonesian shamans sometimes dressed as women, symbolizing by this hermaphroditism their central and mediating role between male Sky and female Earth. Until the nineteenth century the Moslem Sultan of Yogjakarta kept a troupe of transvestite dancing boys to ensure his success in war. Similar examples of Indonesian syncretism could be compiled by readers of Geertz, or indeed by anyone who has visited the islands.

Pak H---, a learned, eccentric and charming sorcerer of modern Solo, studied with sufis in his youth but maintains (along with other informants) that organized sufi orders have died out in Java. He himself converted to Hinduism after reading the works of Guénon, and is now a leader of the almost non-existent Solo Hindu community. Orthodox Hindus would probably find his belief in Atlantis and Mu a bit disconcerting, as well as his claim to practise sorcery.

Pak H--- maintains a picturesque office within sight of the Kraton or Sultan's palace. The royal family is so impoverished that it cannot afford electricity; another branch of the family has sold part of its palace to a hotel.

Solo and Yogjakarta are ancient rivals for cultural and political supremacy in East Java. According to Pak H---, the Sultan of Solo lost his power not only because he sided with the Dutch during the struggle for Independence, but also because he failed in his magical duties. The Sultan of Yogjakarta however was not only a hero of liberation (and until recently vice-president of all Indonesia) but is also a very powerful sorcerer.

Pak H--- shares the Javanese millenarian belief in the coming of a "Just King" (*ratu adil*) who will restore ancient tradition to the island. He says this king will be born in Solo, but only on condition that a certain local volcano be made to erupt—for that is the unmistakable sign or portent which will herald the Just King's birth.

"I have worked for years to bring about the eruption of that volcano," Pak H--- told me, "but the Sultan of Yogjakarta is a potent magician, and opposes me with all his strength."

When I asked why the Sultan should combat such a

desirable cause, Pak H--- laughed wickedly and said, "Because that volcano would destroy the entire city of Yogjakarta!"

The reformist Moslems of Java detest sufism, and the nominal Moslems have turned largely to the religion of pure esotericism, Kabatinan (from the Arabic *baten,* "esoteric"). Kabatinan has no central organisation, but might best be described as a congeries of sects, all distantly related but serving different classes and types of people. Perhaps the best-known Kabatinan sect is Subud, which has spread beyond Indonesia, but hundreds more thrive in Java. High-ranking government figures, including the highest, are known to practise cave meditation and other occult rites, for without some reputation for magic a politician or soldier cannot expect to impress the Javanese.

During the Independence struggle, Kabatinan played a patriotic role. Pamongs (spiritual teachers) are said to have trained their disciples in mystic martial arts that rendered them invulnerable to weapons, and I heard many such stories repeated as gospel in Solo. Moreover, Kabatinan prides itself on its Javaneseness and makes a point of supporting the traditional arts of batik, gamelan, dance and puppetry.

One major Kabatinan group which has attracted a few Western disciples is called Sumarah. In Solo I met a number of pamongs and students and attended meditation sessions which reminded me (with their emphasis on silence and spontaneous speaking) of Quaker meetings. The violent *latihan* of Subud is rare in Sumarah, which prefers to temper inspiration with balance and self-knowledge.   A great deal of Sumarah vocabulary is Islamic, and specifically sufi. *Sumarah—surrender. Iman—*conviction. *Dhat—*essence. *Wahyu Alam—*Nature. *Kolbu—*heart. Other terms are Sanskritic: *trimurti—*body, mind, spirit. *Rasa—*intuition. *Budi—*compassion. *Indraloka—*heaven. Some Sumarah pamongs use a more Islamic approach than others, and pepper their discourse with *"alhamdulillah"* and *"La ilaha illa'Llah."* Sumarah respects all religions, but is not itself an organized faith. Sumarah pamongs are not gurus or mursheds in the sense of absolute spiritual authorities. They are simply guides and teachers. Each seeker must become realized by himself—no one can do it for him.

The contrast between Sumarah and the sorcery of Pak H--- expresses a Javanese duality: the former is cool, subdued, contemplative; while the latter is wild, entranced, magical. But the differences are not all that great. Both paths arise from a melange of religions and cultures, and share many specifically Javanese techniques in common (such as *kunbum* or water-immersion meditation, best practised in lonely jungle pools or under waterfalls). Both owe debts to sufism. Both seem *risky,* sorcery for obvious reasons, and Sumarah because it refuses us the comfort of submitting to orthodox dogma or an infallible master. All Javanese mystics, whatever their path, seem to share a devotion to the Wayang Kulit or shadow-puppet play, and this artform offers a perfect example of syncretism: Hindu epics transformed by sufism into a play of light and shadow (see Chapter Six).

Islam tamed some of Java's native demons, or chased them to Bali. Javanese aesthetic is profoundly compatible with Islamic taste; it is somber and rich in color, elegant, smooth, gliding, subtle, sorcerous but abstract, introspective but occasionally violent, graceful, and addicted to the pure two-dimensionality of pattern. Javanese culture is quiet, and cultivates the art of good manners; it is virile and worships the sword (*kris*); it practises self-denial and voluntary poverty as proof of its nobility.

But some of the primordial demons were never driven out of Java by Islam. To listen to a gamelan orchestra (which one must forever associate with the smoke of clove-scented cigarettes) is to hear the music of the Other World, the Imaginal realm of djinn and spirits. The classical dance, for all its swooping restraint and elegant flatness, continually pulses into magic and hovers on the verge of trance. Somewhere between this shamanic trance-state and the sober clarity of Islam, Javanese syncretism takes on its own distinct and very intoxicating taste.

❀　　　❀　　　❀

Timothy Drew was born to former black slaves in North Carolina near the end of the nineteenth century, and was later adopted into a local Cherokee clan. According to his own account he earned a living after the turn of the century as a circus magician. In the course of his travels he visited Egypt, where he spent a night alone in the Great Pyramid. There he received a revelation which he wrote down and titled *The Circle Seven Koran*. In 1913 he founded the Moorish Science Temple of America in Newark with himself as prophet under the Islamic name Noble Drew Ali.

During World War I the Moors refused to fight for racist America and were persecuted along with other pacifists. Noble Drew taught equality, not hate, but was driven out of the East by the police. In Chicago he began printing "Moorish Passports" and making converts (among them Elijah Muhammad, future founder of the Black Muslims). In 1924 the Chicago Temple was raided in a gun battle by police, and Noble Drew subsequently died in jail, undoubtedly beaten to death. A number of his followers claimed to succeed him as prophet, including his chauffeur. The Science Temple declined in importance in the black community, though it still exists. I had some contact with the Moorish Governor of Baltimore, a poetic white-bearded man whose junk shop smelled of rose attar, in 1966 and '67; and later with younger members of a branch in Brooklyn.

In 1957 an offshoot of the Temple was formed by some white bohemians who had Moorish passports. (Noble Drew restricted membership to what he called "Asiatic races," which included anyone of Celtic descent. White members of the Temple were known as "Persians.") This new splinter group was called the Moorish Orthodox Church of America. Its members were attracted to sufism, and the Temple seemed to them a sort of native American version of Islamic esotericism. These new Moors did not care if Noble Drew stole *The Circle Seven Koran* from *The Aquarian Gospel of Jesus*. They liked the fact that he'd been martyred in the cause of freedom, and they admired him for having the imagination and spirit to found his own religion. Also, it must be confessed, certain Moors of both colors shared a predeliction for certain restricted substances, and an economic interest in their distribution.

The psychedelic movement of the early 1960's brought new converts to the Moorish Orthodox Church in Manhattan, Baltimore and upstate New York. For a number of years an underground temple, headshop and motorcycle garage supported Church activities on New York's Upper West Side. Close connections were formed with Ananda Ashram and T. Leary's League For Spiritual Discovery in Millbrook. Other branches were founded, but only the above-mentioned have persisted for long.

Moorish Orthodoxy, which is now an incorporated religion, has no dogma whatsoever. It is perhaps a loose framework made up of whatever symbols its members find useful, but with a basis in Moorish Science and sufism. (The "orthodox" element is largely ignored.) Within this framework questions are asked but no answers provided. Certain Moors have moved toward sufism or some other "authentic" Islamic esotericism, others have practised yoga, Ceremonial Magick and communal agriculture.

Aside from whatever *baraka* ("blessing") the individual members of the Church may or may not have gained, the M.O.C. itself could be described as a small but perfect example of heresy as a means of cultural transfer. The Moors were part of an attempt to digest and synthe-

size newly-discovered oriental culture with a revolutionary and self-liberating version of American individual-
ism. In this—if in nothing else—the 1960's were a partial
success. The Orient is now taken for granted and has
become mixed into our own cosmopolitan culture. Thousands of translations and studies have opened up the
East, even as its traditional cultures are dying out. No
social panacea, no final synthesis is likely to emerge, but
the experience of the East continues to deepen and enrich
the life of the West. In this subtle and far-reaching
process, "heresy" can play a catalytic role.

❀   ❀   ❀

Forced to accept examples rather than definitions,
and feeling by now perhaps somewhat entangled in a web
of obscure references, the reader may question the utility
of this book. Aside from the dubious and obsessive satis-
factions of collecting and recording little-known facts,
what purpose does it serve to rake up old scandal?

I might attempt an objective answer: Islamic culture
is still too often seen in the West as both monolithic and
shallow. Recently, politically powerful elements within
the Islamic world have deliberately emphasized precisely
the most banal and totalitarian aspects of their own
culture, and as a result anti-Moslem sentiment thrives in
Europe and America. I wish to show that Islamic culture
has in fact been fragmented, divisive, polyvalent, varied,
subtle—a pattern with hidden ramifications; and that
this culture has been complex and creative, not limited to
the monochromatic bigotry of modern Islam.

However, I might also offer a subjective and even an
autobiographical excuse for dealing with aspects of Islam
which others might consider tangential, even insignifi-
cant. I sought out this material, I found it, and now I wish
to present it—at least in part—as an imprint of monadic
consciousness, almost as a Yeatsean persona.

But between the paradox-clashing jaws of objectivity and subjectivity, a more adequate apologia might be conjured up for this book. I spoke of "poetic facts." These may be thought of as Images which store up and release intuitional knowledge. Such a "fact" may be expressed in words, yet still offer an intimation of some reality (*haqiqah*), some realization on a profounder level than that of the "ordinary intellect" (*'aql*).

The "facts" in this book (and some fictions too, perhaps) may prove of very little interest to students of Islam, and may in fact cause offense to many Moslems. It can fairly be said that the book is not really "about" Islam. For me these facts and stories are like bits of a crystal prism which may be arranged in a light-saturated pattern, thus unveiling the very heart of light to the perception. These bits of scholarship, dervish-gossip, old poems and cheap lithographs, half-forgotten fragments of afternoons in cities now half-ruined by war and revolution—all this is meant to summon up a single loose pattern, something like a long poem. If this poem is about anything, it is about *wahdat al-wujud,* the Oneness of Being. Its anecdotes and metaphors and quotations are meant, like images in a poem, to focus and resonate, enhance and clarify this theme—to give it substance, to give it "flesh" through the eros of memory and words—to make it present to the Imagination.

(Note: These essays were written at different times in various places. Parts of Chapters Three and Four have appeared in *Studies In Mystical Literature* in Taiwan; a version of Chapter One appeared in Italian in *Conocenza Religiosa;* some material in Chapter Four (the life of 'Iraqi) was salvaged from a bowdlerization of one of my own books, *Divine Flashes;* a small part of Chapter Six is borrowed from my *Persische Bildteppiche*, which was never distributed in the English-speaking world; and so on. In revising and re-arranging the material for this book I eliminated some but not all repetition, which in any case is an integral aspect of Islamic esotericism and art. I would like to thank Elémire Zolla, Robert Eddy, William Chittick, Bernd Manuel Weischer, Nasrollah Pourjavady and Karl Schlamminger for their help, without in any way implicating them in my opinions or errors.)

2

Secrets of the Assassins

1. A Fatimid Chrestomathy

On the seventeenth of Ramazan, Hasan II—upon whose mention be peace—caused his followers to come to Alamut. They raised four great banners—white red yellow & green—at the four corners of the minbar. At noon he came down from the fortress & in a most perfect manner mounted the pulpit. Baring his sword he cried: O inhabitants of the worlds, djinn, men & angels! Someone has come to me in secret from the Imam, who has lifted from you the burden of the Law & brought you to the Resurrection. Then he set up a table & seated the

people to break the fast. On that day
they showed their joy with wine & repose.

Rashid al-Din

He sacrifices a camel & raises a red
standard, lays castles waste & lifts the
curtain of Concealment which is the
door of the Law. He ought to be called
the Orphan Pearl, for he has produced
bezels on the limitations of Reason.

Haft Bab-i Baba Sayyidna

The same power which appears in sun
moon & stars, that power is in a black
stone, & in darkness. Spirit & body are
complete & perfect through each other.
Separate from each other they do not
exist.

Ibid.

2. The Chains of the Law

Metaphysics abandons the city: all the greystone angels
which decorate the bridge come to life & flap heavily up
into the low mist. Everything on either side of the skin
falls subject to doubt. Quick! reconstruct something to
outlive this betrayal. . .

The cupbearer—call him the Saki for the sake of style—
remains when all else fails; and desire, the unhealed
wound. Sometimes a crack opens between the two, like
the rose I set between myself & the Saki. Everything else
is losing its grip: a spectral flight of luminous gulls across
the low grey sky, over the bridge.

And the Law abandons us, another ponderous escape of stone angels. I have no reason to love the Law—why should I? Must I refuse the wine in the cup & the shaman's embroidered robe, all to pay a price? no realization without Law, sin & hell? the city's redsmoke image!

Now darkness. . . in the darkness appears another angel—no way of knowing if it can be trusted—certainly not carved of stone—it looks like the Saki—it filters into the imagination like trembling smoke. It opens this book, *A Fatimid Chrestomathy:* on a certain day an angelic youth ascended a throne on a mountaintop in lost Persia, announcing that the chains of the Law have been broken.

I have no idea who is speaking, who is being spoken to. I swear by my pen I do not believe or disbelieve. The mist closes over the bridge like tuberculosis.

(London)

3. Eagle's Nest

After the death of the Prophet Mohammad, the new Islamic community was ruled in succession by four of his close Companions, chosen by the people and called the Rightfully-guided Caliphs. The last of these was Ali ibn Abi Talib, the Prophet's son-in-law.

Ali had his own ardent followers among the faithful, who came to be called Shi'a or "adherents". They believed that Ali should have succeeded Mohammad by right, and that after him his sons (the Prophet's grandsons) Hasan and Husayn should have ruled; and after them, their sons, and so on in quasi-monarchial succession.

In fact except for Ali none of them ever ruled all

Islamdom. Instead they became a line of pretenders, and in effect heads of a branch of Islam called Shiism. In opposition to the orthodox (Sunni) Caliphs in Baghdad these descendants of the Prophet came to be known as the Imams.

To the Shiites an Imam is far more, far higher in rank than a Caliph. Ali ruled by right because of his spiritual greatness, which the Prophet recognized by appointing him his successor (in fact Ali is also revered by the sufis as "founder" and prototype of the Moslem saint). Shiites differ from orthodox or Sunni Moslems in believing that this spiritual pre-eminence was transferred to Ali's descendants through Fatima, the Prophet's daughter.

The sixth Shiite Imam, Jafar al-Sadiq, had two sons. The elder, Ismail, was chosen as successor. But he died before his father. Jafar then declared his own younger son Musa the new successor instead.

But Ismail had already given birth to a son—Mohammad ibn Ismail—and proclaimed him the next Imam. Ismail's followers split with Jafar over this question and followed Ismail's son instead of Musa. Thus they came to be known as Ismailis.

Musa's descendants ruled "orthodox" Shiism. A few generations later, the Twelfth Imam of this line vanished without trace from the material world. He still lives on the spiritual plane, whence he will return at the end of this cycle of time. He is the "Hidden Imam", the Mahdi foretold by the Prophet. "Twelver" Shiism is the religion of Iran today.

The Ismaili Imams languished in concealment, heads of an underground movement which attracted the extreme mystics and revolutionaries of Shiism. Eventually they emerged as a powerful force at the head of an army, conquered Egypt and established the Fatimid dynasty, the so-called anti-Caliphate of Cairo.

The early Fatimids ruled in an enlightened manner, and Cairo became the most cultured and open city of

Islam. They never succeeded in converting the rest of the Islamic world however; in fact, even most Egyptians failed to embrace Ismailism. The highly evolved mysticism of the sect was at once its special attraction and its major limitation.

In 1074 a brilliant young Persian convert arrived in Cairo to be inducted into the higher initiatic (and political) ranks of Ismailism. But Hasan-i Sabbah soon found himself embroiled in a struggle for power. The Caliph Mustansir had appointed his eldest son Nizar as successor. But a younger son, al-Mustali, was intriguing to supplant him. When Mustansir died, Nizar—the rightful heir—was imprisoned and murdered.

Hasan-i Sabbah had intrigued for Nizar, and now was forced to flee Egypt. He eventually turned up in Persia again, head of a revolutionary Nizari movement. By some clever ruse he acquired command of the impregnable mountain fortress of Alamut ("Eagle's Nest") near Qazvin in Northwest Iran.

Hasan-i Sabbah's daring vision, ruthless and romantic, has become a legend in the Islamic world. With his followers he set out to recreate in miniature the glories of Cairo in this barren multichrome forsaken rock landscape.

In order to protect Alamut and its tiny but intense civilization Hasan-i Sabbah relied on assassination. Any ruler or politician or religious leader who threatened the Nizaris went in danger of a fanatic's dagger. In fact Hasan's first major publicity coup was the murder of the Prime Minister of Persia, perhaps the most powerful man of the era (and according to legend, a childhood friend of Sabbah's).

Once their fearful reputation was secure, the mere threat of being on the eso-terrorist hit-list was enough to deter most people from acting against the hated heretics. One theologian was first threatened with a knife (left by his pillow as he slept), then bribed with gold. When his disciples asked him why he had ceased to fulminate against Alamut from his pulpit he answered that Ismaili arguments were "both pointed and weighty".

Since the great library of Alamut was eventually burned, little is known of Hasan-i Sabbah's actual teachings. Apparently he formed an initiatic hierarchy of seven circles based on that in Cairo, with assassins at the bottom and learned mystics at the top.

Ismaili mysticism is based on the concept of ta'wil, or "spiritual hermeneutics". Ta'wil actually means "to take something back to its source or deepest significance". The Shiites had always practised this exegesis on the Koran itself, reading certain verses as veiled or symbolic allusions to Ali and the Imams. The Ismailis extended ta'wil much more radically. The whole structure of Islam appeared to them as a shell; to get at its kernel of meaning the shell must be penetrated by ta'wil, and in fact broken open completely.

The structure of Islam, even more than most religions, is based on a dichotomy between exoteric and esoteric. On the one hand there is Divine Law (shariah), on the other hand the Spiritual Path (tariqah). Usually the Path is seen as the esoteric kernel and the Law as the exoteric shell. But to Ismailism the two together present a totality which in its turn becomes a symbol to be penetrated by ta'wil. Behind Law and Path is ultimate Reality (haqiqah), God Himself in theological terms—Absolute Being in metaphysical terms.

This Reality is not something outside human scope; in fact if it exists at all then it must manifest itself completely on the level of consciousness. Thus it must appear as a man, the Perfect Man—the Imam. Knowledge of the Imam is direct perception of Reality itself. For Shiites the Family of Ali is the same as perfected consciousness.

Once the Imam is realized, the levels of Law and Path fall away naturally like split husks. Knowledge of inner meaning frees one from adherence to outer form: the ultimate victory of the esoteric over the exoteric.

The "abrogation of the Law" however was considered open heresy in Islam. For their own protection Shiites had always been allowed to practise taqqiya, "permissable dissimulation" or Concealment, and pretend to be orthodox to escape death or punishment. Ismailis could pretend to be Shiite or Sunni, whichever was most advantageous.

For the Nizaris, to practise Concealment was to practise the Law; in other words, pretending to be orthodox meant obeying the Islamic Law. Hasan-i Sabbah imposed Concealment on all but the highest ranks at Alamut, because in the absence of the Imam the veil of illusion must naturally conceal the esoteric truth of perfect freedom.

In fact, who was the Imam? As far as history was concerned, Nizar and his son died imprisoned and intestate. Hasan-i Sabbah was therefore a legitimist supporting a non-existent pretender! He never claimed to be the Imam himself, nor did his successor as "Old Man of the Mountain," nor did *his* successor. And yet they all preached "in the name of Nizar". Presumably the answer to this mystery was revealed in the seventh circle of initiation.

Now the third Old Man of the Mountain had a son named Hasan, a youth who was learned, generous, eloquent and loveable. Moreover he was a mystic, an enthusiast for the deepest teachings of Ismailism and sufism. Even during his father's lifetime some Alamutis began to whisper that young Hasan was the true Imam; the father heard of these rumors and denied them. I am not the Imam, he said, so how could my son be the Imam?

In 1162 the father died and Hasan (call him Hasan II to distinguish him from Hasan-i Sabbah) became ruler of Alamut. Two years later, on the seventeenth of Ramazan (August 8) in 1164, he proclaimed the Qiyamat, or Great Resurrection. In the middle of the month of Fasting, Alamut broke its fast forever and proclaimed perpetual holiday.

The resurrection of the dead in their bodies at the "end of Time" is one of the most difficult doctrines of Islam (and Christianity as well). Taken literally it is absurd. Taken symbolically however it encapsulates the experience of the mystic. He "dies before death" when he comes to realize the separative and alienated aspects of the self, the ego-as-programmed-illusion. He is "reborn" in consciousness but he is reborn in the body, as an individual, the "soul-at-peace".

When Hasan II proclaimed the Great Resurrection, which marks the end of Time, he lifted the veil of Concealment and abrogated the religious Law. He offered communal as well as individual participation in the mystic's great adventure, perfect freedom.

As will be seen in the quotation at the beginning of this chapter, he acted on behalf of the Imam, and did not claim to be the Imam himself. (In fact he took the title of Caliph or "representative".) But if the family of Ali is the same as perfect consciousness, then perfect consciousness is the same as the family of Ali. The realized mystic "becomes" a descendant of Ali (like the Persian Salman, whom Ali adopted by covering him with his cloak, and who is much revered by sufis, Shiites and Ismailis alike). In Reality, in haqiqah, Hasan II was the Imam because, in the Ismaili phrase, he had realized the "Imam-of-his-own-being." The Qiyamat was thus an invitation to each of his followers to do the same, or at least to participate in the pleasures of paradise on earth.

The legend of the paradisal garden at Alamut where the houris, cupbearers, wine and hashish of paradise were enjoyed by the Assassins in the flesh, may stem from a folk memory of the Qiyamat. Or it may even be literally true. For the realized consciousness this world is no other than paradise, and its bliss and pleasures are all permitted. The Koran describes paradise as a garden. How logical then for wealthy Alamut to become outwardly the reflection of the spiritual state of the Qiyamat.

In 1166 Hasan II was murdered after only four years of rule. His enemies were perhaps in league with conservative elements at Alamut who resented the Qiyamat, the dissolving of the old secret hierarchy (and thus their own power as hierarchs) and who feared to live thus openly as heretics. Hasan II's son however succeeded him and established the Qiyamat firmly as Nizari doctrine.

If the Qiyamat were accepted in its full implications however it would probably have brought about the dissolution and end of Nizari Ismailism as a separate sect. Hasan II as Qa'im or "Lord of the Resurrection" had released the Alamutis from all struggle and all sense of legitimist urgency. Pure esotericism, after all, cannot be bound by any form.

Hasan II's son, therefore, compromised. Apparently he decided to "reveal" that his father was in fact and in blood a direct descendant of Nizar. The story runs that after Hasan-i Sabbah had established Alamut, a mysterious emissary delivered to him the infant grandson of Imam Nizar. The child was raised secretly at Alamut. He grew up, had a son, died. The son had a son. This baby was born on the same day as the son of the Old Man of the Mountain, the outward ruler. The infants were surreptitiously exchanged in their cradles. Not even the Old Man knew of the ruse. Another version has the hidden Imam committing adultery with the Old Man's wife, and producing as love-child the infant Hasan II.

The Ismailis accepted these claims. Even after the fall of Alamut to the Mongol hordes the line survived, and the present leader of the sect, the Aga Khan, is known as the forty-ninth in descent from Ali (and pretender to the throne of Egypt!). The emphasis on Alid legitimacy has preserved the sect as a sect. Whether it is literally true or not, however, matters little to an understanding of the Qiyamat.

With the proclamation of the Resurrection, the teachings of Ismailism were forever expanded beyond the borders imposed on them by any historical event. The Qiyamat remains as a state of consciousness which anyone can adhere to or enter, a garden without walls, a sect without a church, a lost moment of Islamic history that refuses to be forgotten, standing outside time, a reproach or challenge to all legalism and moralism, to all the cruelty of the exoteric. An invitation to paradise.

(New York)

4. The Great Resurrection

It is too easy to write "representationally"—to write sequential and reasonable prose. Finally very little of any importance can be said in that medium since it comes from and directs itself to one section of consciousness to the exclusion of all others. Only *poetry* (including texts to be read as well as texts to be sung) and *story* can address consciousness as a whole—which means that poetry and story are both impenetrably difficult and ridiculously simple at the same time—but never "easy" in the sense of "cheaply acquired".

As soon as an idea or image requires expression in the dry form of prose one can be sure it wants to polemicize, to dualize and to offer discrete definitions rather than a field of perception. The intellect, proverbial one-winged bird, deals from a position of weakness because it demands dogma, and dogma demands defense; and as the samurai know, there exists no such thing as an adequate defense. Slash! and that's the beginning and end of it.

When intellect becomes intuition it sheds prose like a snakeskin. In this sense, art is necessary because it constitutes the only possible language of such a re-birth. As a Javanese pamong once told me, "We must all be great artists."

The problem with the doctrine of Qiyamat is precisely

that it is a doctrine—a means of representing a reality which by definition (or rather by transcending definition) cannot be represented but only present. Poetry and story can possess such presence—or at least point directly to it—while the work of prosaic Reason cannot.

So the rational doctrine of the Qiyamat must contain within itself the intuitional key to its own dissolution—like a tapestry which can be unravelled from one loose hanging thread. The tapestry itself is "unreal", a weaving (*baftan*) as opposed to a certainty (*yaftan*)—whereas the absence of the tapestry is real and "solid" since it unveils reality itself.

Poetry and story, which vanish like a cycle of cat's-cradles into the zero of the circle of logos-thread, can present reality far more effectively than prose. The image, unlike the idea, cannot be defined but must be identified with. The poetic or narrative image is open, like the integrated consciousness. Closed dogmatic systems are composed of ideas, not images.

Since the doctrine of Qiyamat is precisely a doctrine of unveiling it must possess a key, in the form of an image, which opens it. Inasmuch as it consists of a polemic carried out by esotericism (*maarifat*) on behalf of reality (*haqiqat*) as opposed to mysticism (*tariqat*) on behalf of religion (*shariat*), the doctrine of Qiyamat expresses itself representationally, sequentially and reasonably. Inasmuch however as it concerns only reality, transcending all dualism and abstraction, it must center around an image.

Precisely in the story of the Qiyamat such an image is found, and it is also, as it happens, a poetic image (perhaps *the* poetic image in Persian literature)—the image of wine. Note that this is the image of real, actual wine, not the image of the image of wine, as with the orthodox sufis. Religious mysticism must guard the distinction between worldly wine and paradisal wine. For the sufis the power of the image arises from this dichotomy, even though strictly speaking it reduces wine from symbol to allegory. A symbol both is and represents the thing it is: symbol is jam today, allegory is always jam tomorrow.

The story of the Qiyamat however mentions actual wine (forbidden by the Law)—drunk in violation of the Fast, in celebration of the interiorization and abrogation of both Fast and Law—a symbol of the ultimate unity of being. For what could the wine of paradise be, if not *this* wine, here and now? as in the inscription on the gate of a Mughal garden: "If there is heaven on earth surely it is here, it is here!"

The image of real wine further implies the image of actual intoxication. Being-in-itself (and therefore realized consciousness) transcends sobriety and intoxication alike. But this scene of actual intoxication at Alamut offers the key to the Qiyamat doctrine because doctrine by itself is sober and thirsty and needs to be completed in madness—or perhaps "finished off" by madness.

The religious or right-hand mystic must allegorize insanity—by saying for example that the true sanity of the sage appears as lunacy to the ignorant—which is true enough from one point of view—but only from one point of view. Sanity is "Law", and the Qiyamat is about breaking the chains of the Law; and so, from this point of view, it is about actual insanity.

"Actual insanity" of course does not mean clinical mental illness, madness as a disease, as a closing rather than an opening. To the Qiyamat-mystic it means rather the shedding of all received opinion, habit and definition, including that of order itself. From the point of view of order and Law therefore it means chaos, illegality and antinomianism. Reality itself is neither nomian nor antinomian. But esotericism, at a certain level, does imply the reversal of all symbols, the dissolution of all value systems. Here there is no appeal to a "higher order" or "purpose of existence". Shiva dances because he dances. The dance is nature, the dance is destruction to all reason and intellect.

From the point of view of the Qiyamat, the spiritual "station" called Permanence (*baqa'*) cannot be defined as sobriety-in-intoxication or even intoxication-in-sobriety. Permanence goes beyond all such dualistic terms. But what immediately precedes Permanence is Annihilation (*fana'*), in other words intoxication.

Thus the Qiyamat definitely sides with Hallaj against the Junaydi "sober" school of sufism, and declares that intoxication is "higher" than sobriety. Even the sufis give an esoteric interpretation to the Tradition "Do not approach prayer when drunk"—but the Ismailis do not limit this to a passing "state" (*hal*) or even a "station" (*maqam*). They drop the skin of Law entirely because for them intoxication is an attribute of being itself—perhaps one might say the Supreme Face of Being, since beyond the level of Annihilation there is only the faceless light of absolute existence—which "gives back" to everything its solid reality and re-ifies the world. (Samsara is Nirvana.)

This re-ification is Permanence. . . and only the mad drunkard can know it. Of course even Permanence itself is not permanent—there is always yet another unfolding, unveiling, unflowering—but the Qiyamat goes so far as to teach that reality itself is intoxicated. (See also Mahmud Shabstari's *Gulshan-i raz,* a sufi text much read by Ismailis, which describes the drunkenness of the universe and of the angels.)

"Separation" and "Union" are attributes of the lover, not of Love. They are "real" enough, but only when temporally and psychologically defined. From the point of view of reality there is no difference between them.

We are subject as individuals to change, to periods of dryness and periods when no amount of wine will suffice; but this mutability provides no compulsion to adhere to a Law—or a Path—predicated on the supposed virtues of sobriety. In wine is remembrance. Therefore, says the Qiyamat, be drunk as much as you can, in whatever way you can. Needless to say it is not recommending alchoholism or paranoid schizophrenia. But it is also not denying that a good bottle of wine (or all sorts of other "sins" in the eyes of outward Islam) can be an adequate and even necessary support for contemplation.

Does this mean that mysticism of a purely quietistic nature, or indeed religious mysticism in general, somehow falls beneath some supreme level of realization attained by intoxication? "Higher" and "lower" are not the issue; the esotericist can have no quarrel and make no such value judgement about any Path, since all are assumed to lead to the same goal. Where a teaching such as that of the Qiyamat offends against quietism and religion in general is in maintaining that in fact there is no Path at all.

The Ismailis applied their spiritual hermeneutic (ta'wil) to scripture, but they took quite literally such lines of poetry as

Take one step outside yourself—
The whole Path lasts no longer than a step.

(By Shah Nematollah Wali, another sufi much admired by Ismailis.)

Even that single step is strictly speaking non-existent, and there subsists nothing outside the self (or Self if you insist) because the self in and of itself is already the complete and total manifestation of being. On this perception depends the entire micro/macrocosmic esoteric cosmology of Ismailism, as well as the doctrine of the Perfect Man (or Imam-of-one's-own-being).

Of course for not-yet-realized consciousness, the Path does still exist; it can be spoken of as a psychological reality, but not in the strict sense as a spiritual reality. The Qiyamat simply states that one can behave as if reality were One because such in fact happens to be the case. . . so why behave as if it weren't?

Is there no such thing as an esoteric morality? The answer must be no. Pure scandal! Or at least that such a morality can only arise from consciousness and situation, not from diktat. Tantra visualizes this by making "sin" into "sacrament" and by abolishing caste. The Islamic spirit is aniconic and non-representationalist. It is not a sacramental religion. But for the Islamic esotericist a similar attitude, a tantrik *style* must spread out and permeate all of life. One can speak of a tantrik "taste" within Islamic esotericism, found for example in Hallaj's defense of Satan (in the *Tawasin*); or Ibn Arabi's contention that sexual intercourse is the highest form of contemplation (in the last chapter of the *Fusus al-hikam*); or in the use of hemp by "Lawless" dervishes and the Assassins; or in the imaginal yoga of "sacred pedophilia" (shahedbazi, the "Witness game") expounded by Ahmad Ghazzali and Awhadoddin Kermani; or in the cult of sacred kingship in Java where the royalty of the Sunan of Solo (a Moslem ruler) depends on his intercourse with the Goddess of the South Sea. Even some sufis, not to mention the orthodox ulema, have labelled such ideas "innovation" or heresy.

The usual view of antinomian morality is that the realized person can commit no ill act, since illusory ego has given way to a will in harmony with being itself. If "I am the Truth" (*ana'l-haqq*), then what I do is true. Or rather, since there is no true or real thing except truth or reality itself, then all action, all things are one, all things are purified of duality, and hence all are "permitted" (*halal*, ritually pure).

Only fully realized consciousness will be permanently harmonized in this way, and thus safeguarded against any ill action. Those seekers still subject to Separation will of course make mistakes. But even realized consciousness must know pain and suffering. And as for Separation, it is "the will of the Beloved" no less than Union.

The Qiyamat argues that the soul is not liberated if it remains tied to a system which by definition implies lack of liberty, a system with an impossible "catch", a Law. The solution to the paradox, as in the *Chuang Tzu,* amounts to what might be called autonomianism or even anarchism (which is in fact an opening-up of sacred kingship). On the psychological level, such a realization demands a praxis which takes the place of morality in any exoteric sense. Action flows from the still center (*wu wei*) and as such is without limitation or definition. On the separative level it appears to flow towards the center—and thus cannot be impeded or turned back. Mistakes and setbacks, emotions and desires, even pain and suffering are part of this inexorable flow. And if they be experienced as such, all their strength turns to wine, all their bitterness to honey.

The soul can admit defeat—as indeed death defeats it—without losing this inherent realized-ness. Eschatological considerations are negated by Occam's Razor (in other words: there may be an "afterlife" and there may not be; neither case would affect the oneness of being, so the querstion need not be considered). What remains is the "fact" that, whatever conditions and changes consciousness may undergo, consciousness in itself is already free, inalterably perfect, absolutely "void".

The Qiyamat demands that life be lived in this light, on pain of failing to achieve full humanity. This light is the intoxication which informs the very ground of being—and when the 70,000 veils of light and darkness begin to fall, only the drunkard will survive the glare. Does such an esotericism preclude the mystical virtues of serenity, centeredness, compassion, *et al.*? Not at all. But neither does it involve the kind of quietism which accompanies denial of the individuality and the suppression or extinction of desires and emotions. Nor does it call for the ascetic self-denial preached by Law-ful mysticism.

If the wine of this world and that of paradise are one,

it is clear that life without pleasure, without *rasa,* is a "taste"-less and non-human life, spiritual only in the sense that it denies carnality. "It's easy to be a sufi," as one Persian master told me—"what's difficult is to be human." "The sufi is always changing"—"child of the moment." The Qiyamat-mystic opens and surrenders to that change, or rather becomes one with it ("who" is there to "surrender"?) and rides it like a leaf on the stream, or a shaman on a tiger.

If the self is serene and compassionate, so is he. If the self is in love, so is he. If the self is intoxicated, so is he. He can "be with" his emotions, even of anguish and pain, as well as with serenity, violence or compassion—but he will not become stuck in any state or impeded by any concept, structure or event which acquires a false identification with the ego.

He lives life free of false egotism, dessicating rationalism, amputating religiosity or crippling shame. Only forgetfulness or lack of spontaneous attentiveness can deflect him from this course or cause a momentary blockage. And even these lapses can come to serve as reminders-to-remember-the-self, since one cannot help being struck by the difference between "gross" and "subtle" (*latif*) consciousness.

When material rises from the unconscious or "storehouse" it can be dealt with, transmuted into spiritual energy rather than repressed or succumbed to. "He who knows his self knows his Lord" has a psychological as well as a metaphysical dimension. Desire is as much a part of the self as any "pure" awareness; the Qiyamat-mystic can turn the former as well as the latter towards liberation (*moksha*). In following his true nature he follows his divine nature, for to do otherwise would be for him the only possible blasphemy.

If there is no development or becoming in any absolute sense, nevertheless individuals and groups follow each their own subjective arc of spiritual progress.

The Qiyamat was proclaimed in an historical context which equated certain political and social modes with the mystical development of the Alamut community. In the origins of that community lay a concern for Alid legitimacy and a doctrine of "divine kingship".

(Note: This anthropological term ducks the question of Incarnationism (*hulul*) versus Manifestationism. The Nizari Ismaili Imams have never claimed either prophecy or divinity in theological terms—which is why Ismailis are still Moslems. Sufis would say that it is impossible to call the Perfect Man "God" but equally impossible to call him "not-God". In the perspective of the Qiyamat, or of a Hallaj, these distinctions cease to hold any true significance.)

These doctrinal and historical questions continue to concern the Nizaris, who explain that when Hasan-i Sabbah fled Egypt he also arranged for the escape of the infant grandson of the imprisoned Imam Nizar. This child grew up in seclusion at Alamut, which was apparently and openly ruled by the Grand Masters or Old Men of the Mountain. He married and fathered a child who in turn fathered a child who was at first passed off as the son of the current Grand Master, but eventually revealed himself as the true Imam: Hasan II, "upon whose mention be peace."

Destruction of the Alamut library by the Mongols makes it difficult to maintain any historical theories with certainty, but it is widely believed that Hasan-i Sabbah established a hierarchy of initiation of seven grades, the highest of which were freed of the outer Law and allowed to know the true Imam. The proclamation of the Qiyamat would have collapsed this structure—and it is known that by no means the entire community supported the move. Certain conservative dissidents murdered Hasan II. Under his son Ismailism accepted the Qiyamat as an integral part of its teaching, but continued to insist that the true Imam must have as a living "avatar" a Fatimid in the bloodline of Nizar. The doctrine of the Imam-of-one's-own-being was reduced to an allegory, in keeping with Shiite demands and traditions.

Despite his political authoritarianism, perhaps it was Hasan-i Sabbah himself who first taught (to the seventh circle) the doctrine of the Imam-of-one's-own-being. Perhaps to the highest initiates he taught not a legitimist cause but an ultimate spiritual revelation, that of the total inwardness of the Imamate. With this went a political teaching which emphasized the need for freedom from religious and political authority in order to place the teaching within the grasp of those prepared to receive it. Although these politics were "anarchist" from the orthodox point of view, the Nizaris placed an emphasis on the freedom to live a spiritual and "examined" life rather than on ideals of social justice and "primitive communism" in the Qarmatian style. The result was that Alamut was to become a miniature renaissance, a haven for scientists and philosophers living a communal life based on meditation and pleasure, protected by a wall of daggers.

In order to establish this dream as reality, Hasan-i Sabbah found it necessary at first to disguise his goals, or rather to protect them by a series of circles of initiation within the circle of Alamut itself.

By the time of Hasan II the spiritual life within Alamut had ripened to the extent that this Concealment-within-Concealment was no longer necessary. Hasan II offered the gnosis to all his followers, proclaiming an end to the Law but also, by metaphysical necessity, to the doctrine of an exclusively external Imam. It is of no importance whether he was Nizar's great-grandson or not (and in fact the claims for his legitimacy seem to appear suddenly after, not during his lifetime). What is of importance is the realization of the Imam-of-one's-own-being, and the freedom this brings. In other words the

Qiyamat was "anarchist" even from an Ismaili point of view, not to mention the orthodox Shiite or Sunni perspectives.

The reason for Hasan II's murder then becomes much more clear. The "realists" within Alamut had by this time become obsessed with the political success of the experiment, which had spread to a network of mountain fortresses and was growing wealthier than ever on tribute and assassination fees. They had no interest in the unfolding of Hasan-i Sabbah's original spiritual purpose, the creation of a context for the soul's freedom. They feared that their material success might not survive the disappearance of the hierarchy of initiation (in which the lowest rank performed as assassins), or the "democratization" of the Imamate. If everyone in Alamut were to be freed of "duty" how could they be sure anyone would still fight for its political and financial goals? Within a few years they managed to kill Hasan II, pin the blame on outsiders, and explain that the proclamation of the Qiyamat had actually been a revealing of the true (i.e. legitimate) Imam—which was only possible because of Alamut's political and military security. The true esoteric teaching was still available, but once again only to high initiates, not to all who adhered to the Alamut experiment.

This historical scenario would explain the paradox first adumbrated by the late Henry Corbin, that of a sect which approaches true esotericism but then draws back and becomes simply another institution, another structure, another religion. In any case, whatever the "facts" may be, the psychological oeconomy is quite clear: even a tiny elite finds it difficult to escape authority and discover true freedom. Over and over again, mystics who have experienced the oneness of being somehow end by offering schemata which in turn end by crystallizing into literal systems, which must then be re-submitted to ta'wil, penetrated, "bitten through".

Why do so many mystics continue to play the game of

dogmatic structures, ideas and morals, when they have experienced the reality which transcends both structure and structurelessness alike? Why do they proclaim themselves gurus with utter authority over their followers' souls, and why do they themselves submit to religious codes with every evidence of sincerity? Why is a Hallaj or a Kabir so rare? Why must the Qiyamat always be betrayed—or ignored—or hidden away in the shadows of occultism? Is it simply a case of the ego re-asserting itself, or has the traditionalist orthodox mystic actually seen something beyond heretical ken, some ineffable vision of the cosmic police blotter, inscribed with absolutes and punishments and Laws which the more radical mystics have somehow simply missed?

Obviously the orthodox themselves believe this to be the case; and in the end their case boils down to this: After you die your soul is going either to heaven or hell, depending on whether or not you obeyed certain rules in this life, rules which may well have made you miserable, rules which you must never question but only believe to be valid. Whatever visions you experience which may seem to offer freedom from these rules cannot possibly be real "revelations" but only tricks of the devil. Whatever inspiration fails to accord with theology and morality is by definition delusion. Freedom of the soul, they say, lies in submission to these rules, in joyful acceptance of these strictures. Only the Absolute is free of rules, and the relative can never be the Absolute. "I am the Truth" is not to be taken literally. It is only a metaphor. And so. . . Junayd signed the death warrant for Hallaj.

Needless to say, the reconciliation of such an attitude with the pursuit of mysticism neccessitates an intellectual project of immense subtlety, typified by the brilliant contortions of an al-Ghazzali or an Aquinas or a Rene Guénon—but however sophisticated the project the fact remains: you may not drink the wine of this world, and the reason why is a "mystery". Islam is an extreme case, but in the end all religious mysticism comes to this. And in fact religions like Buddhism and Christianity, which begin with much less emphasis on "Law" than Islam or Judaism, nevertheless end with even harsher moral codes. Islam for instance knows nothing of the ideals of monasticism and chastity. Perhaps there is some sort of rule of psychic balance at play here.

Nomian and antinomian mystics agree that the mind needs to be tricked out of its illusory lack of realization. They agree that religious/mystical/ascetic activity provides a barrel of tricks. Wearing a hair shirt, like beating your head against a wall, feels so good when you stop! The sheer relief of it can catapult you into a mystical state. But why must we be so grateful to the hair shirt or to the wall that we carry them around with us for the rest of our lives, perpetuating the ritual of pain?

❁   ❁   ❁

What the Qiyamat suggests, therefore, is not an adherence to a doctrine or dogma or Law, or even to a sect which promises liberation, but rather to the living of a story. Ismaili history is not to be trusted—a tangle of bloodlines and feuds, attacks by ignorant heresimachs. But Ismaili *story* can be trusted whether it is literally true or not, because the very nature of what is taught or told ensures and necessitates a transmutation into "myth". Marco Polo's tall-tale of the drugged devotees is certainly not meaningless, even though told by an outsider. The fable of the childhood pact made by Omar Khayyam, Hasan-i Sabbah and the Nizam al-Mulk is also an outsider's romance, but not without significance. The story that the last Old Man of the Mountain became the wandering dervish Shams of Tabriz (Rumi's spiritual companion) is historically impossible but resonant with hints and clues.

Finally, the most trustworthy stories are those tracable

to the Assassins themselves. The story of the Qiyamat revolves around its central image, the mandala marked out by four cosmic banners surrounding a pulpit. . .the blackrobed figure with raised sword. . .the mountain fortress in the background, umber and ochre and grey. . .the circle of warrior-scholars with their wine-cups, breaking the sacred fast of Ramazan. . .the cobalt-blue desert sky. . .

This mandala breaks loose from the moorings of its historical setting, and even from the text in which it is embedded. It becomes a complex of images, an Emblem, which can be located in the consciousness and expanded, brought to life as an integral element in one's own individual story—the personal myth which always comprises a movement from unawareness toward realization.

Meditation thus becomes narration. The symbols one penetrates make up the path one follows, as with the Grail knights, whose adventures were subjected to the ta'wil of the forest hermits.

The outward physical-historical Alamut, the "hidden garden" where devotees were freed of State and Church, tax, dogma and Law—this image perhaps cannot be imposed on the "real world", was perhaps but a fleeting vision, even in Alamut itself. It is amusing to speculate about the possibility of experimenting with some of the practical teachings of Alamut in the context of today's world. But even if the social freedom of an Alamut cannot be attained, this in no way lessens the importance of the personal freedom granted by the interiorization of the Alamut-story, and of the Qiyamat.

Ultimately society and Law can do nothing to impinge on this freedom—except to hang the free man from a gibbet in Baghdad. You are already free, says the Lord of the Resurrection. So there exists no other story worth living, whatever the risk.

(Suryakarta)

5. Sijil

So he might have said, the Imam Hasan II, Upon Whose Mention Be Peace: "Nothing is true; everything is permitted." This was the teaching of Hasan-i Sabbah, the first Grand Master of Alamut, called the Old Man of the Mountain.

To begin, remember the Testimony of Faith: "There is no god but God." There is no reality but the Real.

"There is no reality. . .": the Negation: all manifestation is unreal. . .

". . .but the Real": the Affirmation through paradox. If only the Real exists then all things partake of this Reality, are this Reality. As Hallaj declared, "I am the Truth."

> All things are but reflections,
> images of the saki's face
> in the winecup
> on the mirror of the wine.
> Knowing this, how can one refuse a thing?

But in the way of the Law it is said, "Some of His manifestations are above others: the talisman of prohibition seals up the cask of wine." In the way of the Path it is said, "One accepts what the Beloved commands, be it Union or Separation."

But for the heart in a state of Union the level of the Law is transcended: A shaykh was once dancing in ecstasy and was repeatedly called to perform the ritual prayer. "I *am* praying!" he replied.

Some will say that only in the state of Union can the seal be broken. Only when no two survive can I say, "I am the

One." Did not Hallaj die on the gibbet?

Hasan answers that "no reality but the Real" negates all states and stations, by relating all separated souls to the one Subject, the Self. Objectively no fragmented self exists to experience or not experience the state of Union. "I" is always in that state. That state is no thing, and that state is true.

Whether the brain knows or not is irrelevant. If one knows, one is a gnostic; but who is this gnostic? No body.

And who is this Nemo who knows? The Imam. Outside yourself you call him Hasan, and mention "peace" upon his name. Inside yourself you call him "the-Imam-of-my-being."

Inside, he abrogates all prescription: "Everything is permitted." Outside, he proclaims the Resurrection, so that the Chains of the Law are broken.

To realize the Imam of one's own being one must begin by acknowledging him. To acknowledge him is to submit to his rule. And his rule—his reality—is "No thing is true; every thing is permitted.'

For the world to continue in manifestation there must exist a living embodiment of this Rule: the Imam seen in the world: Hasan. In relation to you Hasan is the "Beloved", and his Rule brings with it the dispension of an absolute esotericism: the ways of Law and Path become the way of Reality.

But no path remains at all.

Or rather, by the logic of the Resurrection all paths are permitted, valid. Hasan is one symbol of the Imam of one's own being, but other symbols exist, an infinite number of beloveds, of faces reflected in the cup. To penetrate any one of these symbols by taking it back to its source is to realize the Imam. The symbols one penetrates are the path one follows.

In this dark garden, the flowers I
choose
mark out for me a pathway
yet each of these white roses itself
is the object of desire.
My wanderings are guided by you
alone
in whatever costume you
appear;
desire will discover the face behind
the veil,
the mask of saki, flower,
cup or wine.

(London)

6. Assassinations

The houris of paradise are the ideas which at once appear in one's essence when one feels desire. Whatever one wishes—with regard to the perception of the intelligibles—will appear in one's soul, one's essence. Thus shall one be forever in bliss; for the beginning of knowledge, & its ultimate aim, will have become joined together. This is the achievement of the idea of an angel.

Nasiroddin Tusi
The Rosegarden of Submission

He makes one faithful, another an infidel,
he fills the world with tumult & wrong.
Taverns have been edified by his lips. . .
All my desire has been accomplished
through him.

—Mahmud Shabestari
Rosegarden of the Secret

From the moment of the Qiyamat, which by definition stands at a slant to time, "outside" all moments,
Ismaili history and hierarchy themselves fall under the
gaze of ta'wil. Yet another esotericization takes place, and
the whole question of "recognition of the Imam" is trans-
posed to another plane of reference. In the cyclic imagination of Ismailism the absolute and in a sense unmanifest
and unmoving aspect of being is always complemented by
the awareness that being expresses or realizes itself
through change; and that this movement involves, on
both the micro- and macrocosmic levels, a process of
uncovering. In practical terms the process is never-end-
ing—behind the 70,000 veils is no-thing—time and
space describe an arc through curtain after curtain—
consciousness filling itself toward its infinite borders in
the dance of Shiva, Ibn Arabi's "continual creation". To
ride this wave consciously is to possess the prophetic
light—and it is precisely into cycles of prophecy that
Ismaili history divides itself.

The Qiyamat reconciles the basic dichotomy of Islam,
the eso/exoteric, not so much in the sense of a dialectic,
but as the mystically "logical" result of the idea of Unity
(*tawhid*). After Ibn Arabi, there is nowhere else to go. The
ta'wil demands finally that the "secrets" be openly stated,
and since philosophy and outward religion alike lack the
terms of reference to do this, a "new cycle" must be
established.

That the Qiyamat occured when and where it did

historically is of only relative importance, since by definition the "moment" of Qiyamat is outside history, blossom-
ing like a flower from the "nowever", wherever consciousness apprehends it. But in the Islamic context the
institution of a new cycle was of considerable importance.
Men like Hallaj (whom the Ismailis claim for themselves)
had been martyred for their own individual Qiyamats.
The reaction of Hasan-i Sabbah was to withdraw from the
Islamic world both physically in Alamut and spiritually
through *taqqiya* or Concealment. A pyramid of initiation
insured that only the higher adepts knew the "secret",
which involved the dangerous teaching of the abrogation
or interiorization of the Law, and the identity of the
secluded Imam.

Hasan II must have realized that such an occultist
policy only deepens the dichotomy rather than reconciles
it toward Unity, and for this reason he "opened" Ismailism
all the way to the *baten* (the interior, the esoteric) and
dispensed with Concealment. What more he planned at
Alamut will never be known, since in true Shiite fashion
he was martyred within a few years.

By proclaiming the Qiyamat, Hasan II "became" the
Imam—which is no more than to say that he recognized
the Imam-of-his-own-being. Whether or not he was also
the secluded great-grandson of Nizar is without significance in the real context of the Qiyamat. As Corbin
pointed out, it is ironic that this ultimnate esotericism
should in turn become yet another of the seventy-two
sects, with its own dogmas and legitimacies, in a sense
betraying within so few years the meaning of Hasan II's
insight. In the Islamic context, there is always room for
yet another heresy—which is not inappropriate, since
within the human heart there is always time for yet
another unveiling. The historical fate of the Qiyamat is
bound to be ironic, even at times tragic. Its inward significance however escapes all such duality, since it points
directly to inwardness itself, the oneness of being, and is

thus always new and always renewable.

Again, it accomplishes this ironically by the very act of penetrating history—time and space—in the proclamation at Alamut. Something of the same sort happened when Shinran told his followers that the gates of hell were closed not only for those who invoke the Name, but for good and all. Similar teachings were transmitted by the Prophet to his close Companions—but in neither case was the proclamation understood to have abrogated religious Law. Hasan II in effect tells his celebrants at their wine that his word in itself is liberation, for in fact each of them is the Imam. Being is already and in itself perfectly realized. There is no path and no goal for those who adhere to this moment, but only *haqq*, reality itself. The only way out of the paradox is to announce that there is no paradox—like the Zen koan of the goose in the bottle—and this announcement becomes in historical terms the bootstrap by which every succeeding soul desirous of liberation can hoist itself beyond the reach of its own failures of consciousness. Thus the myriad betrayals of the Qiyamat cannot touch it or endanger it; in a sense, they do not exist. Only "salvation" exists—except that there is nothing to be saved from.

The moment of Qiyamat for the individual—or rather the moments of unceasing unveiling—constitute his "visitations" from the Hidden Imam, or Khezr, or Ovays al-Qarani, or the personal guardian angel. Human awareness is structured symbolically and perceives through form. "This," as Ibn Arabi says, "is the vision of God in things, which some say is greater than the vision of things in God." This vision can either be imaginal (such as a vision of Khezr, or of the Qiyamat at Alamut, or of an angel) or it can be actual (as in the "zen" perception of the immediacy of a cup of tea or a flower or whatnot). It can also be both simultaneously, as in the love of the Witness, who is both beloved and angel; or in the recognition of the Perfect Man, the historical "Imam of the Time". In no case, however, is there any question of faith or belief or dogma—only of knowledge (*erfan*), of which the highest form, according to Ibn Arabi, is love.

The historical Qiyamat, then, is a symbol—an imaginal fact—to be contemplated and subjected to ta'wil, used as a focus for perception, a mode of understanding, a means to consciousness. To consider it a religious dogma is simply inappropriate. Rather, it is a gate of perception, permanently open. To walk through it one simply walks through it—and discovers that there was never a step to be taken. The Qiyamat is an affiliation without an organization, a sign for expressing a state of awareness.

There is no question here of the "bondage of form" but rather of liberation through forms; not a "saving illusion" but a reality which is already "saved", from "pre- to post-eternity" as the sufis say. On the psychological level the symbolism of resurrection is obvious: the realized self is twice-born. In the Abrahamic tradition, the doctrine of bodily resurrection is necessary in order to bring theology into line with the absolute demands of Unity. For any non-dualistic metaphysics, even the body must eventually be seen as "real"; even the rankest neo-platonist would have to agree. The myth of the afterlife, therefore, cannot be allowed to "spiritualize" the body into insignificance. Hence the idea of the resurrection of the body. "Even" the body will be reborn into the One.

The Alamut Qiyamat however sets aside all vexed and vexing problems of metaphysics (such as the immortality of the soul and/or body) by declaring that metaphysics and physics are indistinguishable: this body, this soul, here and now, is free. The idea of reward and punishment after death is meaningless in this context, except as a symbol for immediate psychological reality. One is "reborn" into the present, into presence.

Hasan-i Sabbah's famous saying, "Nothing is true, everything is permitted," is on one level an esoteric restatement of Islam's basic assertion, "No god but God"—

or rather, "No reality but the Real." If all that exists is "God", the absolute being, the Void, then all that exists is "no-thing" (or *mu* in the Taoist/Zen tradition)—and if all that exists is God, how could anything be other than permissable (*halal*)? This is the realization behind Hasan II's saying that "The chains of the Law have been broken", for on another level Sabbah's dictum explains the reason for the interiorization of the Law through ta'wil and its consequent abrogation on the material plane. The Qiyamat is quite openly antinomian—or rather a-nomian in essence and scandalous from the point of view of outward Islam. The celebrants drank wine because they were reborn in "paradise", but also to demonstrate that in order to interiorize the Law it is necessary to reverse its symbolism (all symbols are reversable) and actually abrogate it, "break" it. This is the "benign inversion" rather than the "malign inversion" of symbolism, not a demonization but an angelification.

The Law in question is not only religious Law but what might be called the Law of the Ordinary. The shaman knows that freedom is upside-down and inside-out. To realize it, against the sluggish tide of the ordinary, neccessitates a spiritual path of reversed polarities, outrageous trickery and unseemly behavior. Tribal society preserves a sense of the "sacredness" of such reversals. Civilization and outward religion gradually suppress them or evolve a theological mysticism which explains and allegorizes them away.

The final argument of religion, even and especially of religious mysticism, is to point out that most humans are in fact not "realized" beings and therefore must remain subject to Law. To proclaim a Qiyamat—so say the right-hand mystics—violates the actual unspiritual nature of man's lowly and somnolent existence. Finally, it seems, no one, not even the saints, is worthy of freedom. Real freedom, it seems, is found in submission, not to Reality, but to the Law which struggles against Nature for our souls.

For the adherents of the Qiyamat there is no need to engage in polemics, and in fact no vocabulary shared with exotericism in which such an argument might be carried out. The only reply that can be made to orthodoxy and to orthodox mystics is that man is already free, whatever his brain may tell him, and no matter how many times he "forgets". Indeed, the Qiyamat is no more than a reminder, stated by necessity in the baldest, most open and uncontentious manner possible in the vocabulary of the period: that realization is not a becoming but a being. If the soul continually falls back into the structures and traps of dogma and moralism, then it must be continually jolted loose again by "revolutionary" proposals such as the Qiyamat.

No one pins the label "heretic" on himself, for realization is not a matter of being "against" anything. But once it has been pinned, it may come to be worn with a certain pride, not unmixed with a sense of irony. If the heresy then becomes a religion in itself, this does not lessen the spontaneity or beauty or efficacy of the original moment of insight. It is always possible to be one of the people of the Qiyamat. It is not a matter of belonging to a sect, but of having-knowledge (*erfan*); not a matter of history, but of the personal cycle which brings the soul to the land of Hyperborea, ruled by Khezr; or the island of emerald where the Imam awaits his time; the personal moment of awakening into reality, of rebirth in the knowledge of self, of the Qiyamat.

(Penang)

7. Ghazal

The Old Man of the Mountain my child
has faithful servants fanatics of love
drugged with green shadows of paradise.

Climb that cliff he orders them
& at my command leap into the abyss
riding clouds on your rainbow drums

or else fall to your death.
The Old Man in his black silk robe
striding the top of his tower!

Child I will jump without hesitation
without choosing or not choosing. For you
are the Witness at the middle of my night.

Score this song for trebles & organs
like a Mass for the Lord of Earthquakes
& we'll smoke to commemorate my apotheosis.

(London)

3

Eros and Style in
The Interpreter of Desires

1.

She said, "I marvel at a lover of such conceit
        to walk so proud among a garden's flowers;"
I answered, "Do not wonder at what you see—
        it is yourself, in the mirror of a man."*

In his own commentary on this poem, Ibn Arabi
explains that "when a man realizes God in the sense of 'I

---

*Muhyi'din ibn al-'Arabi, *The Tarjuman al-Ashwaq (Interpreter of Desires),*
translated by R. A. Nicholson; first edition 1911, reprinted by the Theosophical
Publishing House Ltd. (London, 1978), poem X, p. 65. [This and all other verse
translations somewhat emended. Unless otherwise noted, all quotations are from this
edition. The poet's own commentaries follow each poem, so I give no references other
than to the number of the poem.]

am His hearing and His sight', this station justifies the attribution to him of whatever is attributed to God." In addressing his beloved, who is identified with God—and who in fact was the fourteen-year-old daughter of a Persian shaykh whom he met in Mecca—Ibn Arabi paraphrases the poem thus: "I am like a mirror to thee, and in those Qualities with which I am invested thou beholdest thyself, not me—but thou beholdest them in my human nature which has received this investiture." And he adds, "This is the vision of God in created things, which in the opinion of some is more exalted than the vision of created things in God."

Ibn Arabi seems to hesitate to include himself openly among those who hold this position—although if he did not think this way, at least during the "spiritual moments" which inspired this poem (and indeed the whole of the *Interpreter of Desires*) presumably he would not have written as he did. The position he so delicately defends is in fact a reversal of the usual formula of a great deal of orthodox mysticism. Taken in isolation it might give weight to the arguments of those who accuse him of pantheism (albeit "monistic pantheism"). Indeed, this seemingly pure immanentism must be balanced against other writings in which he upholds the more usual Islamic mystical position, that the divine is simultaneously Immanent and Transcendent, but that orthodoxy demands a certain precedence of "God the Creator" over "God the inner reality". In short, to see God in things means in effect that anything can be a perfect divine manifestation, and this in turn throws into question the whole concept of Divine Law (which then must explain why some divine manifestations should be forbidden and others permitted). Moreover, it causes problems with the idea of ontological hierarchy: if everything is already perfectly manifested, what happens to eschatology, or to all the "higher realms of being" symbolized or expressed by the heavens, angels, Ideas, etc.?

Ibn Arabi of course has answers to these problems, but the fact that he could make this assertion about "the vision of God in things" reveals a certain very profound shade of difference between the mysticism of his "School" and that of many others, including the neo-platonism which influences most Christian poets, and even many sufi poets. An understanding of this shade of difference will provide the tools for a hermeneutics of the erotic symbolism of his School, and illuminate the importance of style in the poetry of that School.

Inasmuch as religious orthodoxy rejects pantheism, so most orthodox mysticism gives more weight to the vision of things in God than of God in things. A theological mysticism, like that of Dante, has no difficulty preserving notions of forbidden-and-permitted, or higher-states-of-being, because to see things in (or against a ground of) God is by no means to see all things as equally perfect manifestations of God. Ibn Arabi's paradoxical suggestion that the opposite might be the case (or even more difficult, that it might also and simultaneously be the case) needs to be explained by reference to a metaphysical rather than to any theological/mystical position.

Within sufism, Ibn Arabi represents the School of *wahdat al-wujud,* Unity of Being. (This has also been translated as "Transcendent Unity of Being", as if to imply that it is not "Immanent Unity of Being"; but there is nothing of this in the actual Arabic phrase, and it has a touch of orthodox apologetics about it.) Ibn Arabi's position has been admirably studied in T. Izutsu's *Sufism and Taoism,* H. Corbin's *Creative Imagination in the Sufism of Ibn Arabi,* and elsewhere; it would be beyond the scope of the present work to go over the ground again. For the sake of argument, let *wahdat al-wujud* be identified with the Vedantine formula "Thou art That" and the Mahayana assertion "Samsara is Nirvana." To carry this position to its logical conclusion would mean that the platonic "ladder of being" exists only from the point of view of limited consciousness. From the point of view of being itself, there is no such ladder; it has collapsed upon itself into the single point of unitive consciousness. Any "hierarchy" of Being is useful only as a temporary description of consciousness which has not yet "reached" this point ("reached" in quotation marks because in truth there is no becoming, nowhere to "go"). Even separative consciousness, unknown to itself, is already a perfect manifestation of the One—rather, it is the One.

No one can speak of knowing this One, this Essence (*zat*), because "to know" implies knower and known, and Unity of Being precludes any such duality. There does exist such a thing as Annihilation in the Essence (*fana'*), but—as in Attar's parable of the moths and the candle— he who remains within this state "sends back no news". For most mystics, Annihilation must be a momentary experience, still "colored" by the individual archetype— otherwise, no mystic would remain, and no mystery. For this reason, many sufis speak of a "higher" state than Annihilation: *baqa'* or "Permanence". In this state, the mystic "returns' from Unity to multiplicity. If Annihilation is an ecstasy, a stepping outside the body, or form, then Permanence can perhaps only be called bliss (Sanskrit *ananda*), since it involves no such split between consciousness and form.

Permanence is "higher" than Annihilation because it fulfils the very "purpose of creation". "I was a hidden treasure," says God in the Tradition, "and I desired [or 'loved'] to be known; therefore I created the world that I might be known." On the one hand this implies (as Corbin puts it in his *Creative Imagination*) a *deus patheticus* who needs creation (and especially its center, human consciousness) as much as creation needs Him. On the other hand, one can speak of metaphysical "necessity": Being must manifest itself to the fullest extent of its potentiality, "all the way" to the very borders of an illusory "nonbeing". A drama must be played, and played to its conclusion—and the name of the drama is "desire", God's desire to witness Himself, His beauty, in the mirror of creation.

In practise, Permanence is and must be different for each mystic who experiences it. First, its nature or "taste" will be determined by the mystic's individual controlling archetype(s), his "Lord" as Ibn Arabi calls it—his "personal guardian angel". Second, it will be colored by his own soul, his psyche—not the "carnal self", which is in any case illusory, but by his "self-at-peace", his individual human nature transformed or transmuted by the mystical experience, and liberated into the "creative Imagination" which orchestrates for him the play of form and essence. Finally, Permanence will be determined at least partially by cultural and religious forces which have moulded the individual soul and its experience of realized consciousness. The paths leading to the mystical moment are as many as there are wayfarers, but so are the paths leading from it (even though in practise the archetypes or "angels" of culture and religion create certain broad categories).

The "carnal self" or unawakened consciousness is prevented from "seeing God" by the psychic links which bind it to things, and which it interprets as desires. This is a psychological fact recognized by all mystics, and solidified in virtually all religious systems in the form of moral codes which regulate the relation of self to other by making some things obligatory and others prohibited. In Islam, this aspect of religion is crystallized by the doctrine of the divine revelation of Law; the revealing of the shariah, the Divine Law, is qualitatively different from the "revelation"—or more properly "inspiration"—accorded to the individual mystic. This qualitative difference results in a powerful tension in Islamic mysticism between Outer and Inner. In effect, the mystic sees God in all things, but is told by Law that some of these things are prohibited: their "inner" is divine, but their "outer" is forbidden. Islamic mystics may talk all they like about the "superior rights of esotericism", but if they wish to remain within orthodoxy they must admit that in the end it is Law which appears to have the upper hand. Even to say that the mystic participates in the "prophetic light" does not exempt him from Law; somehow the shariah must be accepted as the structure within which the mystical experience is to be contained and interpreted.

In their public utterances, therefore, Islamic mystics tread a thin ice separating mysticism from what would be heresy from the point of view of the exoteric mentality. Some of them fall through—Hallaj, Hamadani, Sohrawardi, the Ismailis—and are expelled or even executed. Others, like Ghazzali, set themselves the task of reconciling mysticism and orthodoxy, a project which involves as much brilliance as tendentiousness.

Ibn Arabi, unlike some of his followers, escaped severe persecution if only because his voluminous writings contain numerous passages which can be interpreted (and rightly so) as representing his own accomodation with orthodoxy. Here however the details of the intellectual and spiritual oeconomy of this accomadation must be set aside in favor of an examination of what might be called his "radical mysticism". Ibn Arabi is like an ocean out of which later mystics have drunk what they wanted. Some of them were actually orthodox scholars, others were Ismailis or "Lawless" dervishes. Others were poets, deeply influenced not only by his poetry but by the metaphysics which informs it. For the most part this poetry represents an expression of the more radical side of Ibn Arabi's work (too huge and varied to be called a "system"), and which is exemplified by *The Interpreter of Desires*. A discussion of the eroticism and style of this poetry must therefore begin with some analysis of this radical aspect of his thought, and the special vocabulary it entails.

For the sake of argument, let it be said that the vision of things-in-God is more congenial to the orthodox type of mystic, the vision of God-in-things to the radical. Obviously such a sweeping generalization will call up as many exceptions as examples, and must ignore infinite shades of the spectrum between a hypothetical black and white—yet in some ways it appears a fair statement.

Suppose a mystic comes out of a tradition, like neo-platonic Christianity (particularly of the Augustinian variety) which expresses a definite contempt for "things". The body is vile, sexual pleasure is vile, Nature shares Adam's original sin. At best Nature can be a symbol of the divine, though in truth more an allegory than a symbol, since it can never be finally and radically identified with the divine. While this position escapes radical dualism, since it admits that "ultimately" Nature is "good" since God created it, such neo-platonism also falls short of radical non-dualism, since it places great emphasis on qualitative differences in the hierarchical structure of Being, and hence on the necessity for the strict regulation of relations between self and other. This relation is thus in some senses a "closed" one. For Christianity there is the added factor of the theological doictrine of the unique incarnation. No thing within the mystic's perception can measure up to this one single historical penetration of matter by divinity. Things, to be seen as good in any sense, must be seen "in" Christ, and as secondary (at best) to His Divinity. "Annihilation" for such a mystic may involve a union on some level with Christ, or the Christic principle. But his "Permanence" must, almost perforce, involve an "abstraction" of things into the divine.

Many Islamic mystics share what might be called the neo-platonic "distrust of things". Human love, for example, can never be more for them than a "metaphor" (*majaz*, or "bridge") for divine love. Such mystics would therefore obviously tend toward the pole of the vision of things-in-God rather than God-in-things. However, Islam completely rejects the idea of incarnation—the doctrine that the divine can be completely identified with any single unique thing in theological terms. It also rejects the idea of original sin, replacing it (at least among the mystics) with the concept of "forgetfulness".

Thus—to oversimplify—individual things possess a certain moral neutrality in Islam (always excepting those which are banned by Law): things can either be experienced as blocks preventing fully realized consciousness, or on the contrary they can be experienced as theophanic in nature, direct manifestations of divinity. Nature, for the Koran, is the greatest miracle: "signs for men of perception" (Koran, XXX, 21). Creation is untainted by "sin"—only man's consciousness determines the relation of self to other. Thus the relation is more "open" than in neo-platonic Christianity.

Islamic mysticism therefore contains a greater potential for the vision of God-in-things, and if the implications of the doctrine of the Unity of Being are followed to a certain logical conclusion, this vision would even seem to take precedence over that of things-in-God. There is no need to "abstract" material creation "back" toward the Godhead; creation is already divine because it is the divine. The locus for the perfect realization of this identity is the consciousness of the realized mystic, he who "sees with God's sight and hears with his hearing" (as in the Tradition quoted by Ibn Arabi). Such a consciousness revalidates or reifies created things, provides as it were a center around which they may dance, freed of their illusory heaviness.

The "radical" position expressed by Ibn Arabi possesses profound implications for two areas of human experience, areas which a certain kind of more orthodox mysticism often seems to call into question, and even at times to denigrate: human love, and art. Ibn Arabi and his School present a high defense of these things, which indeed for them are closely related; perhaps the highest defense possible within the framework of a mystical "system". Unlike much mystical versification which is both fleshless and dull, that of *The Interpreter* exemplifies an eroticism, and an intensity of style, which set it apart even in sufi literature, not to speak of mystical literature in general.

2.

The question whether a given Persian or Arabic poem is "sacred" or "profane" arouses passions even amongst sufis, not to mention scholars and religious authorities. Arabic poets such as Ibn Arabi and Ibn al-Farid, and Persians such as Hafez, Iraqi, Rumi, Jami and Saadi, made consistent use of erotic imagery and references to wine, following in part pre-Islamic literary modes and in part a special sufistic development of purposefully "shocking" themes which play with the tension between inner and outer aspects of Islamic teaching. When Ibn Arabi first circulated the poems in *The Interpreter,* certain exoteric authorities condemned him for the book's blatant eroticism and pronounced it totally profane. As Nicholson points out in his introduction, this reaction seems particularly obtuse in view of the very obvious mystical intention of the work—even without commentary. The author had to flee Egypt in fear for his life, such was the outrage which greeted the *Tarjuman.* In response to this criticism, Ibn Arabi—never at a loss for words—undertook to produce a commentary on his own poems in the form of a line-by-line mystical interpretation of *The Interpreter.* Such a text is rare in sufi literature, and offers a chance to settle once and for all many of the questions raised by the use of erotic imagery in Islamic mystical poetry.

Nevertheless, the answer to the question "sacred/ profane?" is not "either/or", but rather "both/and". Ibn Arabi's predisposition to autobiography allows us to know beyond question that the poems were written to a specific girl whom he met in Mecca in 598 A.H.: the daughter of a Persian Traditionist named Makinoddin al-Isfahani. The girl was Nizam Ayn al-Shams ("Harmony Eye-of-the-Sun"); she was exceedingly beautiful, and was reknowned for her spiritual attainments and eloquence.

"I have put into verse for her sake some of the longing thoughts suggested by. . .precious memories, and I have uttered the sentiments of a yearning soul and have indicated the sincere attachment which I feel, fixing my mind on bygone days and those scenes which her society has endeared to me. Whenever I mention a name in this book I always allude to her, and whenever I mourn over an abode [a traditional device of the Arabi 'ode' or *qasidah*] I mean her abode."

A poet cannot be much more specific than this: Ibn Arabi is talking about a real girl with whom he was really "in love" in all the romantic and psychological senses of the phrase. Nevertheless in the very next sentence he seems to contradict himself:

"In these poems I always signify Divine influences and spiritual revelations and sublime analogies, according to the most excellent way which we [sufis] follow. . . . God forbid that readers of this book and of my other poems should think of aught unbecoming to souls that scorn evil and to lofty spirits that are attached to the things of Heaven! Amen!"

Nicholson's comment on all this is perhaps typical of the desire most readers feel for an either/or explanation of mystical love poetry:

"If Nizam was to him (and manifestly she was nothing else) a Beatrice, a type of heavenly perfection, an embodiment of Divine love and beauty, yet in the world's eyes he ran the risk of appearing as a lover who protests his devotion to an abstract ideal while openly celebrating the charms of his mistress."

⁎ 76 *⁎*

In other words, Nicholson is satisfied that Ibn Arabi's love for Nizam was purely "platonic"; moralists may be satisfied that he not only never consummated his love, he also felt no physical desire for her. She was merely a "type", an allegory. He could as easily have invented her, only there happened to exist a sweet pious girl named Nizam who happened to provide a convenient hook on which to hang his mystical sentiments.

One does not have to be a modern psychologist to find this interpretation as distasteful as it is suspect. In fact, we have Ibn Arabi's own word for it, expressed repeatedly throughout the book, that he found Nizam physically attractive and that he loved her passionately; and while it is undoubtedly true that the love was not consummated, this is no reason to insult the poet's humanity by turning him into a mere sentimentalist. Note that when Ibn Arabi defends himself against "aught unbecoming to souls that scorn evil" and so forth, he does not condemn physical desire. Indeed, it seems clear that what he denigrates is the petty moralistic point of view that finds such desire incompatible with spiritual experience. In his *Fusus al-hikam* (see Bibliography) Ibn Arabi offers an interpretation of sexuality as the most perfect mode of contemplating the divine, a discourse that would be immediately understood by a Hindu tantrik: "When a man loves a woman, he seeks union with her, that is to say the most complete union possible in love, and there is in the elemental sphere no greater union than that between the sexes. [Man's] contemplation of the Reality in woman is the most complete and perfect. . . .Contemplation of the Reality without formal support is not possible. . . .Since, therefore, some form of support is necessary, the best and most perfect kind is the contemplation of God in woman. The greatest union is that between man and woman." [*fasl* XXVII, Austin's translation]. Whether Ibn Arabi enjoyed such a union with Nizam is beside the point (except inasmuch as the book is about desire rather than fulfilment, a matter which will need further elucidation). What Ibn Arabi wants us to realize is that in Mecca in 598 A.H., Nizam was for him both a girl he loved and the embodiment of divine beauty. For him this love is not in any exclusive sense of the term a metaphor (although it includes metaphor); if his love is symbolic, it is because a true symbol both represents and *is* the thing it represents.

In order to make this paradox as clear as non-poetic language can make it, certain key passages in *The Interpreter* might be underlined and analysed. It is impossible to be systematic about this, since Ibn Arabi himself was the most unsystematic of authors, and appears not only to leap from point to point in hyper-intuitive fashion but also to contradict himself constantly. The following passages, then, are a rough mosaic, meant to suggest rather than delineate in any prosaic and dogmatic fashion, a teaching about love which emerges like flashes of lightning rather than the steady glow of a philosopher's lamp.

❀   ❀   ❀

"Inasmuch as the spiritual element in man is always governing the body, it can never contemplate that which is uncomposed apart from its body and independently, as some sufis and philosophers and ignoramuses declare. Hence my disunion will never be repaired: I cannot become united with Him who is pure and simple, and who resembles my essence and reality. So longing is folly, since this station is unattainable, but longing is a necessary attribute of love, and accordingly I cease not from longing." (p. 59)

❀   ❀   ❀

. . .After the circumambulation we meet,
   our trysting place the well of Zemzem
beside the midmost tent
   beside the rocks.
There those emaciated by anguish
   are brought back to health
by that love-desire stirred in the soul
   by perfumed women who when they feel fear
   let fall their hair
hiding themselves in their tresses
   as in robes of darkness. (VII)

Apparently Ibn Arabi refers to a meeting with Nizam during the ritual circumambulation of the Kaaba, one of his favorite spiritual exercises. The mingling of vision and desire he symbolizes as a vision of angels, creatures of the *barzakh* or world of the creative Imagination. In his own commentary he says:

"Whoever loves these spiritual beings dwelling in sensible bodies derives refreshment from the world of breaths and scents, because the spirit and form are there united, so that the delight is double. When these phantoms fear that their absoluteness will be limited by their confinement in forms, they cause one to perceive that they are a veil which hides something more subtle than what thou seest, and conceal themselves from thee and quit these forms and once more enjoy infinite freedom."

In other words, those who are caught in the aridity of separation are restored to clear perception by their very desire for union; the perfumed women are the personifications of these desires; desire is an angel. It plays on the border between form and formlessness, now bending toward the world of form and bathing it in theophanic light, now toward the world of Being itself, and pure consciousness.

o o o

I, tender and passionate, rolled my cheek
in the dust; by the love I owe you
do not reduce to hopelessness a man drowned
in his own tears, burned in sorrow's fire.
Would you kindle a flame? Look no further than
this smouldering heart. Here, take it. (VIII)

o o o

At al-Abraqan flashes of lightning gleamed
and between our ribs thunderbolts exploded
clouds shed themselves in rain on meadows
and on trembling branches bent toward you.
Gullies flooded, breezes blew perfumes
a ringdove fluttered, a twig sprouted green.
Crimson tents were set up between rivulets that
crept like snakes; tents for sweet women
who sat there bright-faced, rising like suns
large-eyed, noble, well-born and graceful.
(IX)

In the commentary on the phrase "bright-faced", Ibn
Arabi explains that

"there is no doubt of them, as the Prophet said,'Ye shall
see your Lord as ye see the sun at noonday when no cloud
comes between.' "

o o o

Doves that haunt these trees take pity
nor multiply my pain with your lamentation.
Pity! nor uncover with your murmured tears
my hidden desires, secret sorrows.
Morning and evening I answer her with the cry
of a yearning man, moan of passionate lover.

_ 80 *_*

Spirits face each other in thickets of trees
    that bend their branches toward me with
    gestures of annihilation
offering me varied tormenting desires
    passions, untried afflictions. . .
Often they swore themselves changeless but
    those beautified by henna do not keep their
    word
and of all marvels the foremost is that veiled
    gazelle
    who points with henna'd fingers and winks
    at me
a gazelle who pastures between breastbone and
    guts—
    miracle! garden amidst fires!
My heart is capable of every form:
    pasture for gazelles, convent for monks
idol-temple, pilgrim's Kaaba
    tables of the Tora, book of the Koran.
I follow the religion of love: where its caravans go
    there is my faith, my religion. (XI)

Ibn Arabi comments:

"The aspirations and desires of all seekers are attached to her, yet she is essentially unknown to them;
hence they all love her, yet none blames another for loving
her. Similarly, every individual soul and the adherents of
every religion seek salvation, but since they do not know it
they are also ignorant of the way that leads to it, though
everyone believes that he is on the right way. All strife
between people of different religions and sects is about
the way that leads to salvation, not about salvation itself. . . .She manifests herself everywhere, like the sun;
every person who beholds her deems that she is with him
in her essence, so that envy and jealousy are removed
from their hearts."

When Ibn Arabi says that his religion is love, he is not talking about some aimless generalized sort of *caritas,* but about *eros;* and this is so because he sees God in the girl he loves, not in an abstract principle. Religions deal in abstractions rather than in the thing itself; those individuals who see and "taste" the palpable manifestation of the divine no longer care to quarrel over vague generalizations.

> He saw in the East lightning and longed for the
>> East
>>> but if it had flashed in the West he would
>>> long for the West.
> My desire is for lightning and its glimmer
>> not for this place or that, nor for earth.
> East Wind handed down a Tradition
>> relayed from Distraction to Passion to An-
>> guish to Pain
> from Intoxication to Reason to Yearning to Ardor
>> from Tears to Eyes to Fire to my Heart:
> "She whom you love is between your ribs
>> tossed by your breath from side to side."
> I told the East Wind, "Send her a message,
>> say she has set a fire in my heart.
> If it is put out—everlasting union. If not—
>> no blame to the lover!"

Here Ibn Arabi satirizes the usual form of a prophetic Tradition, handed down from So-and-so to So-and-so. His informant the East Wind is ordered to take a message to the beloved (a common trope in Arabic and Persian love poetry): if the fire of my desire is put out (by consummation, presumably) I shall acheive total union; if not, still I am not to be blamed, since it is her decision, not mine. The commentary explains that the first lines refer to the vision of God in created things, the manifestation in forms; the poet cleaves to phenomena because the manifestation appears in them; he desires the forms inasmuch as they are loci for the theophanic experience. A chain of spiritual experiences leads him to the realization that his own heart is the only stage where the play of love is performed. Finally in his rapture he reveals that the last lines can mean just the opposite of what they seem to say:

"If the awful might of this manifestation shall be veiled through the permanence of the divine substance, then union will be lasting; but if the manifestation be unchecked, it will sweep away all that exists in its locus, and those who perish are not at fault. This is the saying of one possessed and mastered by ecstasy."

❀   ❀   ❀

> Star-watcher, be my intimate companion—
>   spy on the lightning, my nighttime friend.
> Sleeper by night who welcomes sleep
>   you are tomb-buried before your death
> but if you had loved this girl
>   she would have brought you happiness, bliss,
> and you would have given fair women
>   the wines of intimacy, talked secretly with
>   suns,
> flattered the full moons. (XVI)

He who accepts the ordinary cycle of waking and sleeping as the full range of consciousness inhabits a mausoleum of unawareness. One must pay attention to the lightning and comets of non-ordinary "nighttime" consciousness; one must love. Here Ibn Arabi seems to speak quite openly of Nizam, simultaneously the human and divine beloved, saying of her in the commentary, "though she is unattainable, yet through her manifestation to thee all that thou hast is baptized for thee, and thy whole kingdom displayed to thee."

In the next selection the reference to the "real-life"

Nizam is quite unmistakable, as is the mystical symbolism. The *coincidentia oppositorum* of the lovers mirrors the alchemical process by which the apparent duality of spiritual and human love is reconciled.

> Long have I longed for a tender girl
> > endowed with prose and poetry, eloquent in
> > > her pulpit
> a Persian princess from Isfahan
> > that most glorious of cities—
> she the daughter of Iraq, daughter of my shaykh
> > I her opposite, a child of Yemen.
> My lords have you ever seen or heard
> > of two opposites united?
> If you'd seen us at Rama, offering each other
> > cups of passion without using our hands
> passion making us converse, sweet and joyful
> > without using our tongues
> you would have witnessed a state in which
> > understanding vanishes:
> Iraq and Yemen embracing. (XX)

In one of his most open and daring passages, Ibn Arabi explains the "pulpit" as "the ladder of the Most Beautiful Names. To climb this ladder is to be invested with the qualities of those Names. 'Eloquent' refers to the station of Apostleship," so that she who speaks from this pulpit is identified with the *insan al-kamel,* the Perfect Man; "I allude enigmatically to the various kinds of mystical knowledge which are under the veil of Nizam, the maiden."

❁ ❁ ❁

> ...In my heart, fire of passion
> > in my mind the full moon of darkness sets.

O musk! full moon! branches above the dunes!
    how green the branches, bright the moon,
        fragrant the musk!
O smiling mouth whose taste I loved!
    saliva, redolent of white honey!
Moon that appeared to us veiled
    in the very blush of shame upon its cheek!
Had she unveiled, what torment!
    and for this reason, still veiled. (XXV)

According to the Tradition, "God has seventy thousand veils of light and darkness; if He were to remove them, the splendors of His face would consume all that His sight perceives." Therefore, says Ibn Arabi,

"He keeps Himself veiled in mercy to us, in order that our substance may survive, for in the survival of the substance of phenomenal being the divine presence and its beautiful names are manifested, and this is the beauty of phenomenal being; if it perished, thou wouldst not know, since all kinds of knowledge are divulged by means of forms and bodies."

❀   ❀   ❀

Between Adhri'at and Busra I saw a girl
    of fourteen rising like the full moon
exalted in majesty above Time,
    transcending it in pride and glory. . .
You are a pyx of blended odors and perfumes
    a meadow of spring herbs and flowers:
beauty in you reached its utmost limit—
    another like you is impossible. (XL)

Quoting Ghazzali, Ibn Arabi points out that "a more beautiful world than this is not possible. Had it existed and had God kept it to Himself, He would have shown avarice which is incompatible with His liberality and weakness which is contradictory to His omnipotence."

In one mood, swooning eroticism, Ibn Arabi can write a line like

> Bees compete with one another when she spits.
> Lord, how cool that sweetness. (XXX)

In another mood, mystical speculation, this image becomes an allegory on the realized man and the logos. Both moods are true, but there is no reason to suppose that the poet was unaware of the irony involved in comparing a pubescent girl with the Supreme God of the Koran. He even offers complex numerological proof that fourteen is the perfect number. To such ridiculous lengths a besotted lover will go, he seems to say; and why not? The truth he offers is a kind of madness, and cannot be spoken in prose.

3.

Human love—indeed, human sexuality—is accepted by Ibn Arabi as real; and since it is real, sacred. Even in the few selections given here it must be apparent that the intensity of erotic feeling is not feigned, nor contrived for effect, nor made up solely to point a moral, however mystical. And yet it would be equally wrong to assume that his own commentary, however abstract it may sometimes appear, was concocted merely to satisfy the tiny souls of censors, however powerful and dangerous they might have been. "Mere" human love, Ibn Arabi admits, is limited—yet worthy of the utmost respect, since it is created in man's heart by God to demonstrate the power of emotion which religion, by itself, fails to instil. Even mysticism by itself, he seems to imply, is less worthy than love by itself, since it leads to dry abstraction; he might have quoted the Koran: "Which of thy Lord's blessings will you deny?" (LV, 13). But by juxtaposing poems and commentaries, poetic mode and prosaic mode of consciousness, it is possible to see the full reality of love as he experiences it—a reality which is totally concrete, having nothing to do with bloodless theological idealism. Such a love denies nothing of passion, nothing of desire, nothing of the fleshly and psychological complexity which the human soul can encompass. It does not "use" the beloved as some sort of respectable but out-worn theme for meditation, to be transcended as soon as possible in favor of a vague religious ecstasy. But Ibn Arabi does insist that love, like the prime matter of the alchemists, can be "worked". Without violating its human origins it can still come to englobe the deepest spiritual experience of which the heart is capable. It can do this because in fact it already is divine; because human beauty, in and of itself, is "in the image of God."

The Interpreter of Desires, for all its apparent lack of any systematic approach to an actual spiritual technique, suggests by its violent and original mingling of "sacred" and "profane" the method by which the theophanic apotheosis may be attained. By the use of the creative Imagination, human love, with all its "changes" and "moments" and "states" of anguish and fulfilment, is to be experienced as the exact mirroring of the relation between human consciousness and divine consciousness. (Or rather, since there is ultimately only one consciousness, speak rather of a relationship between two aspects of being, a personal/individual aspect and the unapproachable essence of the Unity of Being.) In this kind of mysticism there is little or nothing of the static, rigid, ascetic or quietistic—nothing abstract. "Separation" and "union" are both accepted as valid, just as the romantic lover accepts without question the beloved's moods of coquettishness or generosity. Indeed, as Ibn Arabi implies, separation is in some senses to be preferred to union, since from the psychological point of view it intensifies and prolongs the purity of love, the "beginner's mind" (to borrow a phrase from Zen) in which the still unsatisfied lover knows the fiercest and most potent states of ardent desire, in themselves a kind of fulfilment; while from the metaphysical point of view, this separation allows the real purpose of the drama of manifestation to be played out, as if God, masked as both lover and beloved, tricked himself into believing that some sweetly poignant gulf separated himself from himself: Narcissus yearning for himself in the mirror of Nature. "Lover, beloved and love: all one," as the fifteenth century sufi Shah Nematollah Vali put it. And yet, if this oneness were ever to be finally and completely realized, creation would cease to exist, and with it all pleasure as well as pain. Bhakti yogis say, "Sugar is sweet; but who wants to BE sugar?" In Ibn Arabi's system, one is the cake, and eats it too.

If mysticism is defined solely as a means for escaping pain and suffering, then evidently Ibn Arabi is not a mystic. And if mysticism is merely the negation of all human emotion, then *The Interpreter* does indeed deserve to be condemned by orthodox authority as the work of a salacious heretic. In effect, mysticism has been so defined—not only by its critics but even by some of its proponents. Gnostic dualism, for example, is the total opposite of everything Ibn Arabi stands for—and yet it too proposes itself as a kind of mysticism. Certain kinds of Buddhism come close to this Gnostic negation, in mood at least if not in metaphysical application. Extreme forms of neo-platonic Christianity and even a great deal of sufism would have to ignore the *Tarjuman* or else allegorize it out of existence in order to accept it. And for the most part, these forms of mysticism have been openly anti-love-and-poetry, or have glorified forms of love and art that appear highly abstract, almost inhuman, compared to Ibn Arabi's versions.

This situation has led to a critique of mystical litera-

ture which condemns it as misty, affectless and vague—
or at best apologizes for it by saying that by its very nature
it must be read for its content rather than its style. Greek
tragedy, from this perspective, is praised as great art
because it accepts the human condition in all its duality,
pain and suffering as well as happiness and joy; while the
mystical poets are relegated to a minor niche (at least in
aesthetic terms) because they lack precisely this contact
with "real life."

The poetry of Ibn Arabi and some of his more brilliant
successors however presents a very different picture of
the relations between mysticism, love and literary style.
To lack the tragic vision is not by definition to lack contact
with life's "palpable substance"; irony and dualism are no
guarantee of vivid style. The poetry of the *Tarjuman,* as
should be apparent even in the selection given above,
deals with highly concrete imagery in a highly beautiful
manner. Blood, spit, intestines, the pain of desire, the
unbearable nostalgia of memory; the fragrance of an oasis
after a sudden rainstorm, the texture of bare flesh, the
croak of a raven, the startling joy of lightning flashing
over the desert; the dark shamanic ecstasies of the intoxicated visionary, the cool serenity of a shrine deserted by
all pilgrims in the hour before dawn—such images are
welded together by the fire of an inspiration which belongs to the bard as much as to the prophet, to the *vates,*
the primordial and orphic figure who is magician, artist,
doomed lover and saint, all in the same moment of revelation and creation.

To such a mystic, poetry is not accidental but necessary. The Greeks would call him possessed by the Muse;
he has no choice but to speak, and cannot help shaking his
people awake with his call to watch the stars and spy on
the thunderbolts. This poetry in turn arises out of another
necessity, that of love; as Iraqi puts it, no matter how he
resists, with one glance from that Magian child he has
broken all vows and fallen in love again; with one sip from

that cup all his fasting has gone for nothing. Such a mystic is wedded to love, because only in love does his soul live, cleansed of all the rust of forgetfulness. Paradoxically only by total concentration on the beauty of the beloved can he succeed in remembering the beauty of his own spiritual nature; without love he has no Self—only an ego.

Ibn Arabi boasts that he himself is the mirror of the beloved, his human nature invested with divine qualities. Such a lover, like Hallaj, will claim a kind of identity with the Real (*haqq*)—but also with the divine in its primordial fecundity, its creativity. The creative Imagination is the mirror of this divine outpouring, and the mystic who experiences the Real in this sense cannot help but be an artist, whether he "imitates" by creating artifacts, by performing (that is, by remaking his own body) or through the spiritual marriage spoken of in the *Phaedrus*. But for Islamic esotericism, as for the "Church of John" within Christianity, the Word takes precedence; therefore such a mystic is wedded above all to poetry, to the pure unveiling of the logos. For words too are things, not just their pale shadows, and words too are lit from within by the fire of Eros, of the spirit. As a lover must plead for a favor, so this mystic is impelled, by the total interiorization of his craft, to produce poetry in which form is the totally adequate vehicle for content.

Such a poet deals with the concrete or palpable because he sees God-in-things rather than (or better than) things-in-God. For him the state of permanence implies that all things burn with total presence. Not only would he say "no ideas but in things," he might even go so far as to say "no ideas at all" (or as Ibn Arabi put it, "The Archetypes have not tasted of existence"). The tension between inner and outer is for him exacerbated to the point where it must be reconciled by the creation of poem-as-thing, vibrating inside with "meaning" but presenting to the senses only the most perfect of surfaces. For such a poet, style is not merely the adornment of some religious or mystical message. For him (as perhaps for God), style is everything. God does not deal in abstractions, but experiences all things as real, as the dance of energy and void, as pattern of light and shadow, as pure and liberating emotion—the motion of the heart. For the mystic, on his own level of poesis, the experience of eros—both human and divine—impels an Imaginal creation which is the exact reflection of this divine and continual outpouring of form. To analyse the style of such a poet is analogous to the hermeneutical and spiritual exegesis of the symbolic nature of creation itself. Things symbolize the Real but simultaneously they *are* the Real; style embodies content but simultaneously it *is* content.

Nothing could be further from the usual interpretation of mystical poetry. Such assertions raise the possibility of an approach to the study of mystical literature radically different from that current in academic (and even mystical) circles. An analysis of vocabulary, grammar, literary devices and structure might come to outweigh—or at least provide a vital parallel to—any analysis of the metaphysical, theological and historical content of mystical literature, thus bringing us closer to what Corbin called a "phenomenology" of mysticism. But to take such an analysis as an end in itself would be the greatest conceivable offense against the spirit which informed poets like Ibn Arabi and his followers. Finally they demand not that we read but that we live, that we throw away the received text and create our own—a text which is not the product of artifice, however profound, but rather the inescapable result of our own authenticity, the radiation of art from the lamp of the logos which has been lit within us by the realization of love.

4

The Witness Game

Imaginal Yoga & Sacred Pedophilia
in
Persian Sufism

(Poems by Awhadoddin Kermani
translated in collaboration with
Bernd Manuel Weischer)

Contemplation Of The Unbearded

"God is he who manifests himself to the
eye of any lover in the loved one. . . .For
just as no other than God is adored,
since it is impossible to adore any created being without seeing in him divinity
itself. . .so it is also with love: no being

can in truth love anyone other than its creator."

Ibn Arabi

Among certain sufis there exists, or existed, a sort of Imaginal Yoga, based on the symbol of the beloved. "Imaginal Yoga": that is, a spiritual technique involving the contemplation of a form or an object of some sort, and its transformation through the power of the Imagination into the focus of a metaphysical experience.

Love is important in one way or another for nearly all sufis, who accept that God's qualities of love and generosity outweigh his qualities of justice and fear. Aside from equating God with love, sufism offers a general mystical interpretation of the psychological experience of love, for example, between husband and wife, master and disciple, or lover and beloved. Sufism often expresses itself through love poems, and there exists (particularly in the Persian tradition) a type of sufism which explains itself solely in such terms and which has been called "The School of Love".

But the "Yoga" in question is something more specific than any of this. It involves the deliberate and "alchemical" transformation of love, and even of sexual desire, into spiritual attainment, through a definite meditational practise.

The imagery of love in Persian sufi poetry usually rises out of the general mystical and symbolic appreciation of love's spiritual power. But in some cases the imagery refers to a specific practise, which is code-named *nazar ill'al-murd,* or "contemplation of the unbearded."

That is, poetic terms such as love, lover and beloved may refer to "purely spiritual" matters, to man's love of God; or they may refer to "purely human" love; or—most often—to both at once. But in the terminology of certain sufis, these terms may have a more precise reference to the contemplation of the unbearded, or *shahed bazi* ("witness play") in Persian. "Witness" is the technical term for the beloved in this particular meditational form, and *bazi* or "game" is a derogatory term which might also be translated as "play"or "playing". *Shahed bazi* has a scandalous ring to it, and presumably this was so even in the middle ages. (In modern Persian slang the term for pederasty is *bachcheh-bazi,* "child-play".) The Arabic *nazar ill'al-murd* has the same risqué implications; in either case the object of contemplation was usually a young boy, somewhere between the verge of puberty and his first shave.

The Witness Game is a controversial subject. Medieval Islamic society in general, the Legalists and theologians in particular, considered it wrong; they called it unbelief *(kufr)* or innovation *(bida')*—in short, heresy and crime.

Among early sufis who wrote in defense of *shahed bazi* were Abu Abdol Rahman Solami and Ibn Taher Maqdisi; perhaps the best known early supporter of the practise was Ahmad Ghazzali, the brother of the famous "Imam" Abu Hamed Ghazzali. Ahmad was once interrupted in the midst of a meditation by some of his friends. They found him seated in his cell-retreat, staring at a young boy, with a single rose on the floor between them. "Have we disturbed you?" they asked. Ghazzali replied, *"Ay w'Allah!"* ("By God!")—and all the company thereupon fell into a "state'; that is, they attained some measure of non-ordinary consciousness or ecstasy.

An early contributor to the theory of *shahed bazi* was Ruzbehan Baqli of Shiraz. His *Jasmine of the Fedeli d'Amore* is a virtual treatise on the subject. Fakhroddin Iraqi also wrote an important text which bears on the subject, the *Lamaat* or "Flashes" (in imitation of Ahmad Ghazzali's famous *Savaneh* or "Sparks"). (See Bibliography.)

The latest "Classical" sufi to practise *shahed bazi* was Abdur Rahman Jami, the fifteenth century poet and philosopher of Herat. "At the spiritual gatherings which he held," according to his biographer, "there was always to be seen, without fail, a boy most fair of face." Jami, a devotee of Ibn Arabi, wrote, "For those who believe in and have experienced Unity, the perfect being is he whose physical eye recognizes the beauty of God (may he be glorified!) through the appearances of the palpable world, in the same fashion as his immaterial eye contemplates the spiritual appearances of the perfect splendor of divinity."

But the name of Awhadoddin Kermani (d. 1238) is more closely associated with *shahed bazi* than that of any other leading sufi. Many stories make it clear that not all sufis approved of him. On the one hand, he was criticized, even severely, by Baha'oddin Zakariya Moltani, Rumi and Shams-i Tabriz (earlier sufis who spoke against the practise included Mohasibi, Jonayd, Qoshayri, Hojwiri, Abu Hamed Ghazzali and even Hallaj). On the other hand, he was supported by his contemporary Ibn Arabi and also by Sadroddin Qonyavi, who was both a Legalist and a friend of Ibn Arabi. This indicates that *shahed bazi* was accepted by at least some orthodox sufis as a permissable practise.

Texts on *shahed bazi* are difficult to find, since in this case, as the Persian saying has it, "The pen is in the hand of the enemy." Little is known of what went on in the circles of sufis like Kermani, since most of them never wrote, or if they did, were censored. Some of the actual practise of *shahed bazi* can be reconstructed from the *rubaiyyat* or quatrains of Kermani. Although most of them are not very good poetry (at least compared to masters of the form like Rumi and Iraqi), they nevertheless give a clear picture of the rite as well as the theory.

The theory, in the briefest possible terms, is this: Reality manifests itself in the form, in the forms, of Creation. Since Reality is One, all these forms are, objectively speaking, subsumed in that One. Subjectively however the forms are indeed many. To attain the One, he who meditates must meditate on form, since Essence in itself is unknowable. Through the form, the symbol, one comes to realize the Essence, which is the Oneness of Being.

But realizing the Essence, the Transcendent Principle, is only part of "knowing God". For God, in a very real sense, is form. Reality is also Immanent. Each form or symbol on which one meditates is the Beloved. Samsara is Nirvana.

The oscillation or paradoxical harmony between Essence and form is part of the Game. To penetrate the symbol, to "unveil" it or "take it back to its source" *(ta'wil),* is to arrive at God from God by way of God. The Game is a masquerade: Love plays all the roles.

The form or symbol to be unveiled in this way is a theophany or hierophany *(tajalli,* literally, "shining through"). God "shines through" the form. In relation to this form, one behaves therefore as a lover: one desires it, and one may attain from it either "Union" or "Separation", according to one's spiritual station, one's preparedness and receptivity.

Ibn Arabi wrote his *Interpreter of Desires* to celebrate his love for Nezam Ayn al-Shams, the fourteen-year-old daughter of an Isfahani shaykh he met in Mecca. Nezam is for him the focus of a theophanic experience; when she speaks in one of the poems, she speaks as the divine beloved.

> She said, "I wonder at a lover who in conceit of
>   his merits
>   walks proudly among flowers in a garden."
> I replied, "Do not wonder at what you see,
>   for you behold yourself in the mirror of a
>   man."   (Poem XX)

Ibn Arabi comments: "I am like a mirror to you (the beloved), and in those qualities with which I am invested you behold yourself, not me; but you behold them in my human nature, which has received this investiture. This is the vision of God in created things, which in the opinion of some is more exalted than the vision of created things in God." In other words, the realization of Divine Immanence is greater than that of Transcendence; and this greater vision is attained by seeing God in things, in the world, in palpable matter.

Ibn Arabi cleaves to phenomena because the divine manifests in them. "I desire the forms only in so far as they are a locus for the manifestation itself." The beloved is unattainable in herself; that is, God in his absolute Essence cannot be known; "yet through her manifestation to you all that you have is baptized for you, and your whole kingdom is displayed to you by that Essential form."

In fact, knowledge of forms is really the purpose of the spiritual life. According to the *hadith qodsi* (a Tradition in which the Prophet reports extra-Koranic words of God), the deity says, "I was a hidden treasure and desired to be known, so I created the world that I might be known." Ibn Arabi also quotes this Tradition: "God has seventy thousand veils of light and darkness; if he were to remove them, the splendors of his face would consume all that his sight perceives." Ibn Arabi comments: "He keeps himself veiled in mercy to us, in order that our substance may survive, for in the survival of the substance of phenomenal being the divine presence and its beautiful Names are manifested. This is the beauty of phenomenal being. If it perished you would know nothing, for knowledge of all kinds is divulged only by means of forms and bodies."

For many reasons it is appropriate that the form to be loved and experienced in this way should be another human being. All of these reasons can be summed up in the words "God created man in his own image." The human form is the central form of creation; man is God's viceregent on earth, and the most perfect symbol of the divine reality.

This beloved human form might exist in the spiritual world but not in the material world *per se*. Thus the Prophet said, "I saw my lord in the form of a youth," a golden-haired boy in a green silk robe, crowned in gold and seated on a golden throne. The visionary form might also appear as an angel, either in "cosmic form" (immense, winged, radiant) or "disguised" in human form. Or the angel may take the form of a living human being. Sometimes Gabriel appeared to the Prophet as Ziya Kalbi, the most beautiful youth among the Companions.

Finally, the beloved may be another human being. The relationship one experiences with this beloved may be sexual (as ritualized in Hindu tantra, or as discussed by Ibn Arabi in his *Bezels of Wisdom,* where he comments on the saying of the Prophet that three things of this world were dear to him: perfume, women and prayer). However in Islam some love affairs must be by (Legal) definition chaste: all those outside marriage or Legal concubinage.

The Law in itself however does not provide the entire reason for chastity in love. In tantrik terms one might say that chastity builds up a psychic energy which can be turned toward spiritual ends, "sublimed" (in alchemical terms) and used in the Transmutation. The Prophet says that he who loves, but does not speak of it, or take any means to consummate it, so that he dies of it, still chaste, will enjoy in paradise the rewards of a martyr. In mystical terms "death" can refer to the extinction of the separative ego, and "paradise" to the state of metaphysical realization.

Some scholars who have written about love in sufism, and even about *shahed bazi,* have hypothesized a Platonic origin for the ideas and practises in question. Ritter, Nicholson and others seem unable to believe that "mere Moslems" could come up with such exalted notions without Greek help. But the sufis themselves, while they may mention Plato, make different claims: they trace their ideas back to the Koran and the Prophetic Traditions already quoted, among others. Some sufis may comment in a general way on the universality of these ideas, or even trace their spiritual ancestry to Plato (as does the philosopher Sohrawardi "the Murdered One"); but their expositions are always carried out in purely Islamic terms.

If *shahed bazi* is chaste, it must consist primarily of looking, contemplating the face and form of the beloved. This is called the Glance *(nazar);* in support of this terminology, sufis cite the Koran: "Do they not consider *(yanzuru fi)* the kingdoms of the heavens and of the earth and what things God has created?" (VII, 185). Also, they quote these sayings of the Prophet: "Seek good from those who have beautiful faces"; "Three things cool the eyes: greenery, water, and a lovely face"; "Gazing at a comely face is an act of worship." (The last hadith was so suspect in Traditionist circles that some jurists claimed one could invoke the death penalty against anyone who quoted it.)

Omar Khayyam in his *Nawruz nameh (New Year's Day Book)* says,

"The sages invariably regard a fair face as a sign of good fortune, and its contemplation a special privilege. They say that the appearance of a fair face has the same influence on human affairs as a lucky star in the ascendant. By way of comparison they cite the garment which has been laid away in a perfumed chest, and, being impregnated with sweet odors, diffuses incense all around; or the ray of sunshine on the water, reflected in a sunless place.

"The 'fair face' is for the philosophers the sign of the perfection of created things; for the inititate it is the reflection which illumines the truth; for yet others it is the manifestation of truth, which lays bare the truth itself to the eyes of those who seek it, in order that they may be brought back to the true by virtue of its reality."

Another sufi author, Abol Hasan Daylami, gives two definitions of the Witness. In Islamic jurisprudence a *shahed 'adel* or "just witness" is one whose testimony cannot be reproached. The *shahed* therefore is someone (or thing) which informs us of the uniqueness of the artisan who made him (or it). So much even the orthodox can accept. Daylami adds however that for the mystic, the *shahed*/beloved is the highest and most perfect focus for this realization; he is one who "testifies" that he has "recently been in the presence *(mashhad)* of the Universal Beauty and has been set apart by his maker from the rest of his works."

In the *Mashariq* of al-Dabbagh, the author stipulates that the path of sacred love is open only to favorably endowed souls, pneumatic types, the elect of the elect. Most men have limited their religious devotions to idols (and it might be added that the pious and iconoclast montheist can make an idol of his piety). Dabbagh comments that even if many people are prevented by lust from the spiritual contemplation of human beauty, this does not mitigate the fact that the human form represents the highest perfection of divine artisanship. As Mahmud Shabestari points out in his *Rosegarden of the Secret,* if this beauty too is an "idol", then if the Moslems understood the matter in its true light, they too would become "idol-worshippers".

Aside from the Glance, embracing and kissing were also permitted in *shahed bazi* sessions, at least according to one enemy of sufism, Ibn Taymiyya, who notes that "a mystic might kiss his beloved and say to him, 'Thou art God'." Music and dance were also essential elements in the Game which were condemned by many orthodox, even certain sufis.

Awhadoddin Kermani and Fakhroddin Iraqi both, when overcome by ecstasy during the *sama'* ("spiritual concert"), were inclined to rend the shirts of the unbearded and dance with them breast to breast. A scene from such a session appears in a miniature illustrating a manuscript of Kermani's poetry (reproduced on the jacket of *Heart's*

Witness; see Bibliography). The shaykh is whirling around, the long sleeves of his robe fluttering like ribbons, to the music of tambourine and flute. The beautiful son of the Caliph of Baghdad, who had attended the meeting out of curiosity and had threatened to have Kermani killed if the sufi made a pass at him, has instead been overcome with admiration for the man, and is stooping to kiss his feet.

Not unexpectedly, anti-*shahed bazi* writings are voluminous. There is no need to describe all the moral, theological and philosophical weapons leveled against the practise. "Say to the believers that they cast down their eyes and guard their private parts" (Koran, XXIV, 30). The Prophet is supposed to have said that the punishment in Hell for kissing a boy is worse than that for raping one's own mother repeatedly. He is also reported to have said, "Keep not company with the sons of the rich, for verily souls desire them in a way they do not desire freed slave girls."

In his *Talbis Iblis (Satan's Lie),* the anti-sufi Ibn al-Jawzi connects *shahed bazi* to the heresy of *hulul* or Incarnationism, the idea that God is especially present in certain avataric figures. Theologians claimed that the Beatific Vision could only come after death, but the sufis pretend that it can be seen with the eyes; "it is not uncommon for a man to claim that he has witnessed God while gazing at a comely slave boy."

Such a heretic might quote Hallaj:

> "Praise to him whose humanity has manifested
>   the mystery
> of the glory of his radiant divinity,
> and who, since then, has shown himself to his
>   creature openly
> in the form of one who eats and drinks
> so that his creature could contemplate him
> with his eyes, as if face to face."

When Shamsoddin Tabrizi met Awhadoddin Kermani, Shams asked, "What are you doing?" Awhadoddin replied, "Looking at the moon in a bowl of water." Shams demanded, "If you've no boil on your neck, why not look at the moon itself?" This anecdote is usually interpreted to mean that Shams disapproved of *shahed bazi;* but perhaps it might indicate that Shams thought Awhadoddin had not gone far enough toward the position described by Hallaj. Apparently Shams also challenged Awhadoddin to a wine drinking contest in the bazaar, but the shaykh refused to thus become one of the "blameworthy".

Aside from any moral, theological or even mystical arguments against the Glance made by orthodox opponents of the practise, their psychological argument was strong: Glances lead to kisses and embraces, and finally to union. Such is human nature. If sex between a man and a boy is forbidden by Law, then so should Glances be forbidden. If there exist saints who can actually surround themselves with temptation and yet remain chaste, the tension involved in such a situation must still be exceedingly dangerous. When Rumi was told that Awhadoddin kept company with witnesses but remained chaste, he is reported to have said something to the effect that "It would have been better if he'd slept around for a few years as a youth and gotten over it." A contemporary psychologist might take a somewhat similar point of view, if for different motives.

The enemies of the sufis were convinced that more went on at their meetings than dancing and (at the most) a kiss or two. Like psychologists, they saw sex everywhere—and perhaps not without some reason. One sufi, accused by the arch-puritan Ibn Taymiyya of sexual immorality, replied, "And so what if I did?"

Undoubtedly there existed sufis then—as now—who were *bisharh,* "Lawless". Some Orders are known for this, such as certain branches of the the Qalandariyya in India and Afghanistan. Distinctly heretical sects within Islam, such as the Assassins, the Ahl-i Haqq, the Qizilbashiyya, Bektashiyya and Hurufiyya, have used sufi terminology and texts without adhering to the Shariah. Aside from these sometimes antinomian movements, sufism has frequently served as a pose for marginal and even criminal elements within traditional Islamic society.

The defenders of Ahmad Ghazzali, Awhadoddin Kermani, Iraqi and Jami—all of whom are accepted in the initiatic chains of orthodox sufi Orders—make the assumption that these men were not hypocrites (the "proof" being the spiritual quality of their lives and their writings) and therefore if they claimed to be chaste, they were telling the truth. Their acceptance as sufi masters and poets does not depend on the "morals" of sufism, but on a question of spiritual "taste". Sufism as such is not concerned with morals. Orthodox sufis accept the letter of the Law and attempt to live in its spirit. Heterodox sufis maintain that the esoteric spirit abrogates the letter of the Law. But sufism itself is the Path, not the Law, and from its own point of view takes precedence over the Law.

Psychologically, *shahed bazi* is a kind of madness. Its proponents admit this—boast of it, in fact—as readily as its detractors. Kermani states openly that no argument put forth either by theologians or mystics can deter him from his path, his *amor fati*.

As for their sexuality (aside from the question of chastity) neither he nor Iraqi ever apologize. In fact, even the Islamic moralists seem to assume that the desire for boys is natural; religious Law is not the same as natural law. Pederasty, according to the usual view of Islamic society, was never considered as grave a fracture of social mores as in Christian society, even though Islamic jurisprudence condemned it just as harshly as did the Laws of other "Abrahamic traditions".

In societies where women wear sacks over their heads, men tend to give overt expression to natural bisexual leanings. The homosexuality of medieval Persia, and of so much Persian love poetry, lacks to a certain degree the atmosphere of shame and guilt connected with it in other societies. Even handbooks on manners for princes could discuss casually the relative merits of women and boys. The emperor Mahmud of Ghazna was not generally scorned as a sodomite because of his love for Ayaz the slave boy. In fact, the pair became a popular romantic symbol, mentioned in the same breath with Layla and Majnun. In his version of the romance (in the *Savaneh*) Ahmad Ghazzali never once questions whether their love was normal or permitted or not. He simply accepts it, and uses it as the framework for his mystical message. In short, aside from any religious question, pederasty was much more "socialized" (in the jargon of modern sociology) in Islamic society than in ours; and in thinking about the sufi Witness-players we ought not to be blinded by our own society's preconceptions and prejudices.

The ultimate problem for the Islamic moralists and theologians was not pederasty or pedophilia *per se;* they dismissed heterosexuals like Ibn Arabi and Ibn al-Farid with just as much scorn as they condemned Kermani. The real danger in "sacred pedophilia" was the claim that human beings can realize themselves in love more perfectly than in religious practises. This was Kermani's claim, and this is what turned even many sufis against him.

The Rubaiyyat of Witness Play: Commentary on Ten Quatrains of Awhadoddin Kermani

1

You toy with the thought
of falling in love
again

of tumbling under
a lovelock's
spell & sway—
for your monkery
& religious cant
were wasted.
O companions of purity!
Call out for
Witness Play!

Awhadoddin begins by comparing the method of Witness Play with that of the narrowly legalistic and exoteric, and of the religious ascetic. Austerity and self-denial are, for the sufi, means to an end, not valuable in themselves or somehow "pleasing to God." Much more to the point is the actual witnessing of the beloved.

The *shahed* or witness is so called because he "bears witness to" and testifies to the reality of truth (or the truth of reality). He is a symbol of God—but the definition of a symbol is: that which both is, and also represents the thing it is. God himself is the Witness, the one who sees. So by seeing the *shahed,* one sees God. Those who experience love in this way are pure, not just in a legal or ritual sense, but because they participate in metaphysical purity, in the oneness of being.

The idea of "beardlessness" refers not merely to the youth of the beloved, but also to this metaphysical purity. "The true living God has neither beard nor coat," said Rufus Mutianus (a friend of Paracelsus). And this Zen koan refers to the same idea: "That Western barbarian: why does he have no beard?" (The "barbarian" is Bodhidharma, the fifth Zen patriarch, who actually did wear a beard. His "beardlessness" arises out of his Zen nature, which is single, eternally unmanifest, mysterious yet "bare-faced" and totally obvious.)

Awhadoddin accepts the insulting label *shahed bazi* without shame; he even invites us to call out for it. This

Game is like the *lila* of Shiva or Krishna: it is the love-play of the divine.

2

All but the truth:
    forget it all
        tonight
& from this
    union-cup drink wine
        tonight.
You still perhaps
    may reach
        eternal union
if you leap up
    & stir your soul
        tonight.

3

My heart
    press on in straightness
        to the mark
toward your desire
    leaving behind
        the lower soul.
You—the witness
    of all spiritual
        states—
will pass
    through all you see
        to the Witness, the goal.

The symbols that one penetrates are the Path one follows. Renouncing the ego here is not ascesis; the self is propelled upward towards its desired end, drawn by the very beauty of that goal. It passes through the subjective experience of the spiritual states and stations, as a witness of their different marvels and gifts, until it reaches the Witness himself, and realizes that all states and stations are but reflections of that one metaphysical experience. Then one tastes the wine of union, the ecstasy of full realization.

Persian does not use capital letters. Thus in the last line of poem 3, the word "Witness" might just as well have been written "witness". This ambiguity points up the ambiguity of the poem itself: in arriving at the Goal, one arrives "back" at the witness, the human person one loves and is contemplating. There is no "Path"; or rather, the path leads back to where it started: to the symbol, the form, and its direct influence on the heart of the beholder. Some sufis call this experience "idol-worship", and insist that it is the true essence of Islam.

4

My heart does not drift
    by an atom's breadth
        from the witness;
my eyes will not open
    except on the face
        of the witness.
Go busy yourself
    with yourself! Why pick
        on me?
Go your own way.
    I'll have my play
        with the witness.

Awhadoddin expresses not merely his desire to be united with the witness; he also insists that he cannot help but see the witness in all things. "Face" here could have two meanings. In one sense it indicates the outer form, the physical object which we perceive. In another sense it means the essence of a thing, its "true face", its god-ness. Ibn Arabi cites the Koranic verse "Everything perishes except its face" (usually read as "except His Face"); for Ibn Arabi the face of a thing is its metaphysical reality, its "unperishing" aspect. Both meanings are applicable here; in fact, the Janus-like oscillation between the two meanings defines precisely the Game itself, the constant play between two ontological levels and one ontological unity.

When Awhadoddin demands to be left alone to go his own way, he is not speaking only to his critics but also to the whole "worldly" world, commanding it to give up its power of delusion and distraction. In this one loses nothing; one renounces not "the world" but merely a phantom; and at once the world is restored in its "pure" aspect, so that all its faces are experienced as the face of the witness. *Maya* is both the veil and the gateway of realization, of *moksha*.

5

> For the witness
>   we'll stake heart & soul
>   on a card
> gamble it all
>   give up earth
>   & heaven.
> In this world
>   what could be better
>   than witness-play?
> Tell me
>   that I may renounce it
>   for love again.

Gambling, like wine, is a "forbidden" image; for Awhadoddin to say that he will gamble everything, his very being, on a love affair, is doubly shocking. To say that he will renounce both this life and the hereafter is only partly hyberbole; the intention behind all these boasts is to demonstrate Awhadoddin's conviction that the technique of *shahed bazi* is the key to metaphysical realization.

To win the bet is to win both the witness and one's own original stake: one's heart and soul, one's rights in this world and the "hereafter" (which is both eschatological and present in the here and now, thanks to the death-before-death of the mystic). By attaining to the witness, one wins a treasure which consists of all that one "renounced", plus all that one desires. Extinction *(fana')* is followed by "Permanence" *(baqa')*, the experience of Reality in the world. One does not lose one's personhood, one's psyche, one's individuality. These are transformed, augmented, irradiated by the light of metaphysical experience.

What possession, then, could be more valuable than the secret of the Game? Could it be, Awhadoddin asks, ordinary piety, or even extreme piety, asceticism, obsessive legalism? Or could it be easy forgetfulness, vain pastimes, wealth, power? Could it even be renunciation itself, or any spiritual state or station? Could it be anything other than the witness, who is both the One itself, and the quintessence of all manifested beauty? No, nothing could have more worth than this secret, the codename of which is Love.

6

How unsplendid:
    a dance where
        no music is played!
May fire consume
    all those
        who cry us blame
for music & dance
    are nothing
        without the witness—

so shame on those
who are not in
the Witness Game!

Most sufis accept music and dance as part of the spiritual path (for a defense of music against its exoteric critics by Ahmad Ghazzali, see Bibliography). Among those of the "School of Love" the *sama'*, or spiritual audition of certain kinds of music, sometimes accompanied by dance, becomes an essential rite. The Mevlevi version developed by Rumi and his followers is perhaps the best known, but is very formal compared to the sort of sessions one pictures through the poetry of Iraqi and Kermani.

I am not sure that such a version of *sama'* still exists anywhere today. I imagine it like this: a small group of dervishes, sometimes wandering Qalandars, sometimes the literate elite of an urban Order, would gather for the rite. The scene might be someone's private *zavieh;* or, as in India today, by a saint's tomb or a remote green corner of a cemetary. (The closest I have ever seen to a Kermani-style *sama'* was the *'urs* or death anniversary at the shrine of Mahdo Lal Husayn in Lahore near the Shalimar Gardens. But although the right sort of people were there—intoxicated fakirs and transvestite dancers—it was more a public festival than a private gathering. Lal Husayn was a Moslem Qalandar who loved a Brahmin boy named Mahdo. They are buried in the same grave. [See Chapter Seven].)

Neither in Classical times nor today would such a meeting ever take place in a mosque; hence the constant opposition of "tavern" and mosque in sufi poetry of this type. The dervishes would either be musicians themselves or would engage professional but spiritually sensitive musicians to play for them. Also present would be one or more young boys of great beauty. The affair was devoted to ecstatic dancing of a more or less impromptu nature, but probably following certain basic forms, which would differ from place to place and be based on what seemed psychologically and ethnically appropriate. Miniaturists loved to show wild dervishes whirling round and round, the long sleeves of their robes flying out like wings.

According to the sufis, the "right" sort of music is that which is attuned to the rhythm of the *zekr,* the invocation of the divine Names. Sometimes this relation is explicit, and expressed directly through rhythm; and sometimes it is implicit, and expressed through melody. The aim of the music is to impel the hearer toward a spiritual experience, and at the same time to embody that experience, to give it audible form. In Awhadoddin's method, the experience was given an even more explicit form: human beauty as a direct reflection of divine beauty. Such a "love affair", tuned properly through music and dance and the images of poetry, will metamorphize the soul, and turn the heart in ecstasy toward the real.

Such practises seem to have prevailed in certain circles of the Sohrawardi Order among spiritual descendents of Ibn Arabi and Ahmad Ghazzali; also among the Qalandars, who were sometimes outside the Law, or outside any mainstream of sufism.

Awhadoddin is here particularly fierce toward his critics. In fact, he seems to have remained on fairly good terms even with his detractors, but he makes clear in his poetry his total commitment to his own path. The shame, the impurity, is in the minds of those who reject this intoxication, which for Awhadoddin is the highest form of religious life.

7

A heart
in love with him
finds no rest

*** 112 ***

discovers
at the door of the witness
its nest & goal.
In short
a sufi meeting
without a witness
is like an idol
made without
a soul.

The attainment of the witness is both a completion and a perpetual striving. There is never enough wine. But there is the experience of coming to rest at that doorway which connects the two worlds, the two levels of manifest and unmanifest, and makes them one.

If, as Shabestari says, true Islam is idol worship, who is the idol? That which we love and worship may be anything, so long as it serves as the focus and form of "meaning" (mana'). Such a symbol is like a temple in which the Presence abides. Temple and idol are one, like a body and its flesh; or like a burning coal and fire; or like a rose and its perfume. An idol without a soul is maya (in the sense of "delusion"); but if the world is realized as possessing a soul, it becomes a "true" idol temple, where the mystic may worship. For Awhadoddin, a sufi meeting which did not allow the Witness Game would in effect outlaw the witness himself (or "Witness Himself"); such a rite is no more than empty posturing—or, at worst, "blasphemy".

Of course, this is hyperbole. Awhadoddin did not literally believe that his way was the only way. To a mystic, such an idea would in any case seem illogical. He merely uses a rhetorical device, to defend his way in ringing terms, to assert that—for him—it is the best path. But more than that: for Awhadoddin the path is the Witness Game, the Witness Game is the path. All paths are witness games—if they are true paths. Awhadoddin is arguing not for a right, or a rite, but for realization. This is made clear in the next poem.

8

> Do not believe
> they chase
> inworldly images
> those who search
> forever
> for the witness.
> That grace
> through which he gives
> a heart its peace
> that grace we call
> (in mystic's tongue)
> the witness.

This is the highest form of the play of witness and witnessed, beloved and lover. The search for the witness is aimed not at mere allegory, or experience, or pleasure, or religion, or even at "mysticism". Its goal is reality itself.

Seen from "God's point of view", reality is one. But seen from "the creature's point of view", reality has a hierarchical structure: that is, some aspects of reality-as-many are more central, more important, more potent, to certain seekers at certain times. According to Iraqi, all things are manifested equally by the One, but some things are manifested-as-forbidden, and those things are prohibited by Law. Some things, again, are central all the time, and these are the avatars, the relatively total manifestations of the divine in this world. Anything which can thus play the role of the symbol which ilumines and liberates us, whether temporarily or permanently, is a "grace of God" (in theological terms). This symbol *is* the witness. It may be a human beloved, or a spiritual teacher, or a religious teaching, or practise, or an *ishta devata* of some kind or another; or it may be a cat, as the sufis say. The important thing is that it provides for us the link between heaven and earth. Just as angels intermediate between man and God, so does this symbol intermediate for us. The symbol is our angel. But more: the symbol is for us the face of God.

9

In the tavern
    we make our ablutions
        only with wine.
A reputation
    once shot forever
        is never reborn.
Our honor's curtain
    is ripped to such
        ragged shreds
I fear it can never
    be made again
        untorn.

For Awhadoddin, the liberating symbol took a form which most of his contemporaries considered improper, if not downright immoral and illegal. This he found ironic, funny—and part of the Game. It is not surprising to find him using the image of disgrace and lost reputation; no doubt, it had certain autobiographical resonances. But he is not merely discussing his social status.

Metaphysical truth is scandalous; that is, it violates all the accepted modes of perception, all the ordinary, epistemologically neutral expectations of the sleeping soul. It tears open a curtain and reveals the occult; it unveils a beauty which is "forbidden" only because we ignore it in our stupor.

Among the sufis, one attains purity not by ritual ablution, not by faith and worship, not by deed or merit,

* 115 ***

but by direct knowledge, experience, certainty, the drunkenness of ecstatic realization. Only this intoxication truly purifies the soul, because with this "wine" one becomes lost, and finds oneself, within the heart. One loses all separative delusions, the dirt of a muffled consciousness, and attains the One.

This is to wander nude in the bazaar, like a naked Qalandar. But if the bazaar is shocked, then scandal belongs to the bazaar, not the dervish. Like a drunkard, the sufi loses his reputation in the world because the world has lost its reputation with him. The petty bazaar stands accused of hypocrisy; the naked man stands before God.

10

> In passion still
>   we orbit
>   round the moon:
> the Unknown One
>   knows of the track
>   we tread.
> We are amazed
>   to find the sane
>   still sober—
> but they are much
>   more perplexed
>   to find *us* mad!

In the angelology of Avicenna and Sohrawardi the moon is the sphere and rank of the Archangel-Intelligence called Gabriel *(Jibra'il),* the Angel of Humanity, the Soul from which all humans derive their souls. Gabriel is then in a way the archetype of the beloved. As planets orbit round the center of the universe, so do souls revolve around this Angel-beloved, the witness.

According to this angelology, the force which causes

the spheres to rotate is the "desire" which the Angel of the sphere feels for its presiding Archangel-Intelligence, who represents God on that particular celestial level. This desire also animates human souls, which are like angels drawn to archangels, or planets toward their stars. Love, then, is the binding power of being, on every level of reality. In fact, love *is* being and reality: love turning toward love in love with itself. Everything is on this track, and everything is being/consciousness/bliss, whether it "knows" itself as such or not. But the soul which awakens and finds itself in the dance: that soul has won the bet.

To follow this dance, this path, is by extension to arrive at its center; there is only one center, God the unknown and unknowable, who yet manifests in the forms of creation, who *is* creation.

But Awhadoddin will carry out this project with "passion". Not merely his intellect nor merely his emotions will be involved, but his entire being. All his faculties will be cooked in this athanor; and in the alembic a Stone will be distilled which will be madness, lunacy.

One may say that the "mad" mystic is truly sane, the only truly sane man in a world of sadly "normal" people. For to be normal in the worldly sense is to be insane, deranged.

But it is not enough to say that mad is sane and sane is mad. For, inasmuch as words can convey the meaning, there is something mad about the metaphysical experience. There is a kind of cosmic playfulness about the deepest levels of reality which, as Chuang Tzu realized, approaches the most chaotic and primordial of essences. "Sanity" is too cold a word, too rational a word to describe this experience.

Moreover, there really is something mad about Awhadoddin's own path, about this *shahed bazi*. It is like an irruption of that primordial and purified madness onto the plane of ordinary daily half-life. To make a passionate rite of such a crazy Game is to set up a whirlwind, a vortex through which everything present, all society, Law, ritual, music and dance, will be sucked into the Other World. It is to create a point, a lamp of metaphysical madness on the dark surface of the "earth"—our sleeping consciousness.

A man who has "been there" steps back into the world perplexed to find that so many conscious beings remain somehow unaware of how totally their earth has been transformed. Why are they not all reeling with joy? Yes, says Awhadoddin, I am mad. And that is precisely what must perplex someone who has never tasted such a wine.

The Platonic Witness

In Plato, especially in the *Phaedrus* and the *Symposium,* certain parallels with the treatment of love in Kermani and Iraqi can be discerned. Socrates speaks of an ecstatic voyage to the "realm of the gods", to the very point of contact with divine reality. Such a voyage reveals for one the archetypes, the Ideas. (Since our Game-players, like Plato, fixed their gaze on young boys, it is tempting to look for philosophical similarities as well—and some do indeed exist.)

When the Platonic visionary beholds a human being who reminds him of the Idea of Beauty, he falls in love. His soul strives after the soul of the beloved just as it flew after the god's chariot. The desire he experiences is like the yearning of the soul for its lost wings. If it were possible, the lover might worship the beloved as a god. In the *Symposium* we learn from the reported speech of the seeress Diotima that this experience of love is only the first step for the soul. From the particular it must come to love the general, and from the general it must come to love the universal, the Idea itself.

In Platonism, material reality is a dim and distant reflection or shadow of the Idea, of spiritual reality. The world is not "evil" (Plotinus defended this point against the Gnostic Dualists) but it is at the lowest reach of the Good. One rises by stages toward the Good, and the purpose of the material world (or a human beloved) is to "excite" the soul toward this ascent.

In sufism (of the kind we are discussing), Plato's love-journey of the soul would be accepted as a beautiful myth and as profound psychology. However, the sufis would bring to it a certain metaphysical vision, derived from Ibn Arabi, Hallaj and other sources, which would cast the story in a new light.

For this metaphysics, Platonic emanationism does not quite do justice to the immediacy of the idea of the unity of being *(wahdat al-wujud)*. The world "comes into being" because it *is* being. Neither "creation" nor "emanation" describe this truth. The sufis prefer the word "manifestation" or *tajalli*, "shining through". Ontological hierarchy exists only from the relative point of view of manifestation; in an absolute sense, all is one. It might be said that the ladder of the Platonic ascent exists only so long as one has not climbed it. To reach the top is to find yourself back at the beginning again, for all journies end in a single point, which is everywhere.

Granted that the Platonic view and the sufi view are different versions of the same thing. But the sufis would say that their metaphysics completes Platonism, or at least complements it. Sufism closes the circle begun by the divine ascensions in the *Phaedrus* and in Diotima's speech, by uniting the realities of Idea and image, meaning and form, shadow, light and archetype.

For Platonism, the world is valuable because it can remind us of higher realities. In the sufism of Kermani and Iraqi, the world is valuable because it can be irradiated by the divine oneness, it can become an idol temple where every idol is God.

The inspiration for this metaphysics comes from the Koran and from the teachings of the Prophet, which emphasize *tawhid* (Unity) in an almost Vedantine way.

But the inspiration for the experience of love comes from love itself. Religion and metaphysics alike crackle and melt in its fire. It is a dangerous game, but he whose eyes are open to the witness wins the highest of all stakes: the witness himself.

Appendix:
A Ghazal by Awhadoddin Kermani

Angelfaced dictators! Cheats
     can be faithful (sometimes)
& if they cause us pain, sometimes as well
     they sell the balsam.
It may please an earthly king
     hunting from time to time
magnanimously to set free
     the game he's trapped;
so give me a glance my friend
     remembering how it behooves the generous
now & then to cast for God's sake
     an eye on the foolish weak.
Untie those lips & give me
     one kiss—or sell it!
(Pleasure should be freely given—but
     sometimes it pays to buy.)
Nostalgic desire in a loving heart
     struck with tender passion
is usually repressed—though sometimes
     one can cure it.
Reputation, wealth, power!
     What harm can befall these
if now & again they remember
     a humble beggar?
If my heart feels drawn to beauty
     don't reproach it—after all,

is that pleasure not known from time to time
        even in your city?
And if perhaps a rumor of me
        finds its way to your ear,
never mind. Even kings may accidentally
        think of rogues & bums.
O marvel! no sin can touch you,
        sweet infidel Chinese boy,
for even those on the path of righteousness
        are capable of mistakes.
Awhad, do not curse your fate
        if that "friend" forgets you—
for who am I that anyone should ever
        remember *me*?

5

The Wine Songs
Of Fakhroddin Iraqi

Fakhroddin Ibrahim al-Iraqi was born near Hamadan (in present-day Northwestern Iran) in 1211 and died in Damascus in 1289; he is buried next to Ibn Arabi. His master was Baha'oddin Zakariya Moltani, head of the Sohrawardi Order, and he also studied under Sadroddin Qonyavi, the friend and interpreter of Ibn Arabi; as a result of these studies he composed his *Lama'at* in imitation of Ahmad Ghazzali's *Savaneh*. He was considered by many to have inherited the mastership of the Order, he was admired and protected by princes and caliphs, and is respected as the author of one of the loveliest divans of Persian poetry. More is known of his life than of Awhadoddin Kermani's, and the following anecdotes of Iraqi reveal important aspects of the biography of a Sufi who believed

in and practised some of the ideas discussed in the last
chapter.

❀   ❀   ❀

"At the age of five", his father said, "the boy was sent
to school. In nine months he had memorized the entire
Koran, and in the evenings he would recite in a sweet
voice the portion which had been his task that day,
sometimes weeping, until all who heard his melodious
voice grew sad and restless. Our neighbours were fasci-
nated by him, and could hardly wait each evening for his
recitation. A group of children, too, had lost their hearts to
him, and he to them. He could not rest quiet one moment
without them. Each day when they were free of school,
they would run off after Iraqi. By the time he was eight he
was famous throughout Hamadan. Every day after the
afternoon prayer he would recite from the Koran, and
great numbers of people would gather to listen."

By the age of seventeen Iraqi had learned all the
sciences, both the transmitted (such as Koran, *hadith* or
traditions of the Prophet, and jurisprudence) and the
rational (such as logic, principles of jurisprudence, philosophy, mathematics, etc.), and had already begun to
teach others. One day it happened that a company of
wandering Qalandars came to the city. (Such figures can
still be seen in Persia, Afghanistan and India. They are
religious mendicants, sometimes rather irreligious, and
dress colorfully in robes sewn with patches. They carry
axes and begging bowls, and either grow their hair and
beards very long, or shave themselves completely.) They
began to hold one of their meetings, and with sweet
melody to chant the following verses:

We've moved our bedrolls from the mosque to the
    tavern of ruin;

we've scribbled over the page of asceticism and
    erased all miracles of piety.
Now we sit in the ranks of lovers in the
    Magi's lane

and drink a cup from the hands of the
    dissolute haunters of the tavern.
If the heart should tweak the ear of
    respectability now, why not?
for we've raised the flag of our fortune
    to high heaven.
We've passed beyond all self-denial, all
    mystical "stations",

for if all of them were pressed together in
    one wondrous cup—we've drained it!

Iraqi beheld this wild crew, and among them he spied
a young boy of unequaled beauty, a boon to lovers' hearts.
If the artists of China had seen those twining locks, they
would have been astonished. Again Iraqi, like an eagle,
stared at the boy, and the bird of his heart fell into the
snare of love. The flame of desire caught at the haystack of
his reason and consumed it. He tore off his turban and
robe (the dress of a theological student) and gave them to
the Qalanders, saying

How if my bosom friend, my beloved,
my intimate, how sweet, if it were you.
        If you compounded a medicine for my
           heart,
           racked with pain, if you cured my soul,
           how sweet.
I would swell so with joy the earth could not hold
    me
if for just one moment you would drink my desire.

My affairs are difficult, but how simple
this business would be, if you'd mix
yourself in it.
Let the whole world declare war on me,
what would I fear, with you to defend me?
Like a dawn nightingale I weep and
weep at a perfume
which hints that you might become my
rose.
Should I ever describe the beauty of a face like a
moon
or refer to cheeks traced with tresses, I'll write
of you
and whether I mention your name or no
you'll be the target of all my words.

I—Iraqi—am binding my heart to you
for I want you, you, as my beloved.

After some time, the Qalanders left Hamadan and set
out for Isfahan. No sooner had they vanished than Iraqi
was overcome with longing for them, and for one in
particular. He began by throwing away all his books:
From all of Razi's *Great Remembrances* all he gleaned
was forgetfulness!
As for *Grammar,* he declared it yammer!
Avicenna's Allusions he branded delusions!
The Signs of Exoteric Revelation became *The Mysteries of Esoteric Interpretation!*
As for Razi's *Structures*—he dissolved them!
As for *The Compendium of Details*—he overlooked
them!

And the tongue of rational discourse he transmuted
to the language of spiritual ecstasy. In short, like one
already detached from the world, he set off in pursuit of

those wanderers, and had walked two miles when he caught up with them. Whereupon he recited:

I have seen that the lane of piety stretches out,
    far, far into the distance;
My dearest boy, can you not show me then
    the way of the madman?
Bring me a glass of Magian wine
    that I may drink deep
for I have given up all thought
    of ascetic piety;
or if the pure wine has all been downed
    bring me the cloudy dregs
for even thick residue lights up the heart
    and illuminates the eyes.
Tuppence for the sufi meeting house!
    I flee the company of the righteous;
fill up a row of glasses with wine
    and bring me the first.
I carry no gold or silver
    nor heart nor religion—
only the eternal triangle of Love
    and the wealth of Poverty.
All fear of God, all self-denial I deny;
    bring wine, nothing but wine
for in all sincerity I repent
    my worship and hypocrisy.
Yes, bring me wine, for I have
    renounced all renunciation
and all my vaunted self-righteousness
    seems to me but swagger and self-display.
Now for a time let my proof be wine
    against the sorrow of Time
for only in drunkenness can one be free
    of the hour's grief.

Once I am thoroughly drunk, what difference
    if I end up in a church or in Mecca?
Once I've abandoned myself, what matter
    if I win Union—or separation?
I've been to the gambling house and seen
    that even the losers there are pure;
I've been to the monastery and have found
    no one but hypocrites.
Now I've broken my repentance, at least
    do not break our covenant:
at least welcome this broken heart and say
    "How are you? Where have you been?"
I've been to Mecca, to circle the Kaaba
    but they refused me entrance
saying "Off with you! How could you dare
    to defile such a sacred place?"
Then, last night, I knocked
    at the tavern door;
from within came a voice: "Iraqi! Come in!
    for you are one of the chosen!"

The Qalanders received him with great joy. At once
they sat him down, shaved his hair and eyebrows (an
offense against pious custom) and, in short, made him one
color with themselves. He continued with them on their
wanderings through Persia, and eventually to India.

❖   ❖   ❖

When Iraqi met his master, Shaykh Baha'oddin, for
the first time, he ran away from him in fear of the fate he
represented. But at length he returned.

At once the Shaykh directed him to make a forty-day

retreat, and set him in a cell. For ten days he sat, and saw no one. But on the eleventh day, overcome by ecstasy, he wept aloud and sang:

First wine that filled the cup
    they borrowed from the saki's drunken
        eyes
and finding revellers still possessed of selves
    poured out the bowl of selflessness.
What fell in the grail from his
    redstained lips they called love's wine
and of his dark curls made a net
    for the hunt of the hearts of the world.
They pounded and mixed the pain
    of the universe and called it "love".
Idols' tresses seem to stir
    like the very souls they agitate.
For drunkards' candies they gather
    pista from lips, almonds from eyes;
from that mouth so to be praised
    the love-sick garner but abuse.
This hall has room for good and bad
    one cup for vulgar and Elect alike;
these glances speak epics to the soul
    these eyebrows signal gospel to the heart.
Lovelocks set a trap
    each breath finds its prey. . .
    Behind the screen discussing secrets
    then openly revealing all—
    They are so free with their treasures—
    why then should they blame Iraqi?

Some of the other dervishes happened to overhear

him, and at once ran and told the Master what was going on. The Sohrawardi rule was strict, and limited its adherents to ordinary pious activities. The other dervishes were already suspicious of the wild Qalander youth, and this new outrage upset them even more. But the master, after listening to their complaints, told them, "Such behaviour may be prohibited to *you*—but not to him!"

A few days later, the chief disciple, Imadoddin, was passing through the bazaar, when he heard Iraqi's poem being chanted to the accompaniment of music (frowned upon by the pious); and passing by the forbidden taverns, he found the same thing: somehow the poem had "escaped" from Iraqi's retreat, and become a hit in the most disreputable quarters of the city. He returned to the Master and reported what he had heard, and recited the whole poem.

"His business is finished!" exclaimed the Master; and he immediately got up and strode to the door of Iraqi's cell.

"Iraqi!" he called, "Do you say your prayers in taverns? Come out!"

The poet emerged from his cell, and weeping laid his head at the Master's feet. But Shaykh Baha'oddin raised Iraqi's head from the dust, and would not let him return to his cell. The youth recited:

In the street of wineshops, when
    should I pray? since my
drunkenness and sobriety alike
    are all the same as prayer.
There, no one accepts the coin
    of righteousness, piety and self-denial:
the only good currency in that street
    is beggary.
None but the drunkard knows
    the tavern's secrets—

how could the sober unveil
    the mysteries of that street?
As soon as I met those
    cunning haunters of the wineshop
I realized that other work than theirs
    is nothing but a fable.
Do you want a guided tour
    of the Mecca of Love?
Come, sit in the tavern, for the trip
    to Arabia is long and tedious.
They refused me entrance at first
    at the wineshop
so I went to the monastery
    and found an open door—but
I heard a voice from within the tavern
    crying "Iraqi!
Open the door for yourself, for the gates
    of drunkenness are always agape!"

At once the Shaykh took off his robe (symbol of initiation, only bestowed on the closest disciples) and dressed Iraqi in it. He also betrothed his own daughter to him, and the marriage was celebrated the same evening. Of this union a son was born, named Kabiroddin.

❀   ❀   ❀

For some years Iraqi rested from his travels in Turkey, where the ruler, the Parwana Amir Mo'inoddin, became his disciple and patron. One day, this same Amir Mo'inoddin came to visit Iraqi, bringing a few pieces of gold. The poet paid no attention to him, and the Amir was somewhat put out. But Iraqi laughed and said, "You cannot deceive me with gold. Send for Hasan the Minstrel."

Now this Hasan was unrivalled in beauty, and had

scorched a great many people with the torch of affection. The Parwana sent for him at once, but when the messenger tried to bring the singer away, a crowd of the youth's admirers blocked their path. The messenger had to return without Hasan, and the Parwana ordered the governor of the province to punish the band of lovers (who are said to have numbered a thousand in all!), with the result that some of them were killed. In the end, Hasan was sent to Iraqi, who came out to meet him in the presence of the Parwana and his entourage.

When Hasan and his friends saw how magnificently they were received, they were astonished, since they had expected punishment rather than honours. Iraqi embraced Hasan and served cool drinks with his own hands. Hasan kissed the dust before the Parwana, and was kindly treated. At last they reached the city, and alighted at Iraqi's hospice, where they began a ceremony of *sama'* (literally "audition": music and dance) which went on for three days. Many fine poems were recited, including this:

> Love the phoenix cannot be trapped
> nor in heaven or earth can it be named;
> no one has yet discovered its address:
> its desert holds not a single footprint.
> The world drains the last drops from its cup
> though the world itself cannot be held in that
> glass;
> dawn and dusk I caress its face, its tresses,
> though where it is no day or night exist.
> Morning-breeze, if you pass its lane
> I have no message for it but this:
> My repose, who are my very life, without you
> I can take no single breath at ease.
> Everyone in this world wants something, but I
> have no desire at all—except your lips;
> from the moment my heart first fell into your
> locks

I've busied myself with nothing but lassos and
   snares.
How lucky to have a friend like you here below
(or Above). . .The enemy hasn't a chance!
Inaugurate a romance then with Iraqi
even though he's unworthy of such a boon.

Eventually Hasan the Minstrel asked permission to
depart, and, it is said, returned home laden with gifts.
   Another day, when the Parwana called on Iraqi, he
found that the sufi had just gone out, and so he hurried
after him. He found Iraqi in the street, where some
children were leading him around by a string, which he
held in his teeth, making him run hither and yon and
otherwise gleefully tormenting him. When the boys saw
the Parwana approach with his retinue and train, they
fled. A few people who heard of this incident criticized
Iraqi, but the Parwana defended him and silenced his
detractors.
   Once, as the Parwana was passing by a polo-field, he
found Iraqi, mallet in hand, playing with some beautiful
boys—as if he had made his own heart the ball for the
mallet of their lovely tresses. The Parwana offered to join
the game, and asked, "What position shall I take?"
   Silently, Iraqi pointed off down the road—and the
Parwana went sadly on his way.

❀　　　❀　　　❀

   In Egypt, Iraqi won the favor of the Sultan by proving
himself an honest man; presumably the Sultan did not
meet many in his daily life. Iraqi's behavior scandalized
the staid muftis and mullahs of Cairo. However eccentric
the sufi seemed, however, the Sultan still believed in his
saintliness, and even went so far as to appoint him Chief
Shaykh.

The poet however continued to act in a way which not everyone would have thought proper for a Chief Shaykh. Every day he used to wander through the bazaars and streets of the city. Once he was passing by a shoemaker's shop when his gaze happened to fall on a lovely boy. He stepped up to the shop, made his salaams, and asked the shoemaker who the boy might be.

"He is my son," the merchant replied. The Shaykh caressed the boy's lips and said, "Is it not cruelly unjust that such lips and teeth should be the companions of shoeleather?" (for cobblers used to have to clench bits of donkey hide in their mouths while they worked on it with their hands). The father replied, "We are poor folk, sir, and this is our profession. If he does not take leather in his teeth, no bread will pass his lips!"

"How much does he earn each day?" asked Iraqi.

"Four dirhams," the cobbler answered. So the Shaykh commanded that each day eight dirhams should be sent to the father, and that the son should work no more. Every day Iraqi and his companions went and sat by the shoemaker's shop, where they would sing and recite poetry and invoke while Iraqi took his ease and gazed upon the boy.

Iraqi's enemies reported all this to the Sultan. He asked, "Does he take the boy home with himself at night?" They answered, no. "Does he remain alone with him in the shop?" Again they had to admit, no. So the Sultan ordered that Iraqi's daily allowance be increased by five dinars.

Next day Iraqi came to see the Sultan and asked why the extra money had been alloted. The Sultan apologized and said, "One has heard that the Shaykh has an expense at the shop of a certain shoemaker. This small sum, one hopes, will help balance your accounts. If you desire," he added, "the boy can be brought to your hospice."

"No," the Shaykh replied, "we must obey the lad. He cannot be commanded."

II. Winesongs

1.

I turned my face to the tavern again
& again fell into its trap.
   How many times did I repent?
   & now for one sip, fallen again,
with the lees of the Magian's cup
broken my fast again.
   In a corner of the inn I saw
   a child of the fire-worshippers;
captivated by his face I stared
& dropped my eyes & stared again.
   With a hundred tricks I saved
   my heart from the webs of love
& now with one glance at that
Magian boy I have lost it again.
   I did not need to see his face
   & already I was doomed
for life without his face is a
dry affair—better be dead again.
   The sadness of love assaults me
   & again I am joyful;
the black bile of love sickens me,
I cast to the wind my heart & faith.
   My virtue & self-restraint destroyed,
   I am washed with corruption again.

  My non-being has some value but
  my being is simply a naught.

  While Iraqi exists he is the seeker—
  when he comes to nothing, he is the Sought.

2.

The saki comes from behind the curtain, cup in hand
    tearing apart the curtain, breaking my vows of
      repentence.
At the sight of his face I go insane. Then
    since I have vanished, he comes & sits with me.
His curls unravel a knot, my heart ascends
    but its life remains far from earth, tangled in his
      hair.
Bewildered I lie in the trap of his locks
    intoxicated with his ruby cup.
My heart caressed his ringlets,
    lost itself, drowned in amazement.
Chained in his dark tresses,
    freed from the world, released from life,
I begged him to free my heart from his curls;
    in reply he laughed & took my head as well.
I sat with him but my heart arose
    beyond earth & heaven, then came to life again.
With one glance I am drunk, with the next sober—
    at the sight of his wine-red locks do I live or die?
I want to sing, to reveal the secrets;
    I am not afraid of anyone, for I am drunk.

3.

I every sweet face I see him revealed,
in every dark eye the liquid beauty;
when I am Majnun he is Layla—
in every lover's sight the beloved,
heart's balm of the wounded, sharer of grief,
help of the helpless, everywhere only he,
he the desire of bewildered lovers,
of all things the goal of my sorrow,

near & far nothing to see but
always he, always & only he,
sole comforter of pain, sole desire,
sole object, I see him alone,
I see the rose in gardens, deserts, wastes:
he is the garden, he the desert;
ha! my mad heart, walk proud to the tavern
for in every cask & glass there is naught but he;
in taverns & gardens drink wine, bright wine,
& smell these roses & lilies which I swear are he!

> Come to the winehouse of the saki
> pour out cup after cup
> pass beyond extinction
> then look for Iraqi—
> for Iraqi is HE!

4.

No wine, saki, no wine?
then give me tears of blood.
> No, give me wine—my liver
> feels like kebabs on a spit.
No, these are the dregs of sadness,
of separation from you, of desolation.
> Light my heart with the fire of wine
> that I may turn my face from the world.
My purse is empty. I know
you will give me nothing to drink
> but be generous. I am the dust
> at the tavern door.
Remember me. Let me
have just one glass,
> one sip. For just one moment
> deliver me from being. . .Iraqi.

5.

The tavern doors swing wide;
drink, my heart. Wine unravels all knots.
        Stare not at yourself but
        at the idol's flower-lidded eyes.
Forget the Kaaba:
the vintner's gates are open.
        Come out, see the beloved's face;
        leave the house: the garden is unlocked.
One atom of one tip of one hair
of one curl explodes in galaxies
        when tresses are brushed from your
           face
        like the locks of night from sleeping
           earth.
A spring of light pours on the earth's eyes
breaking the seals of life from dark roses;
        screens of verdigris are folded back
        from hidden flower beds
tempting my petal-white love to walk
in the garden of contemplation.
        The point of light in the winecup
        tears the curtain of the sun;
the cypress bows before
the laughter of the rose.
        On every verdant lawn
        the perfumer's tray is displayed
that the breeze of dawn may scatter
its scent to the horizons
        ruffling the beloved's curls,
        spilling the musk-bag of Tatary.

        Last night the wind whispered: Iraqi,
        close your door, for the door of the Friend is
        open.

In jealousy he sews shut others' eyes
then opens the lid of his secret treasury.

6.

All soul delicate grace my child
more dear than life my boy;
                 sweet thief of hearts
                 hearts lean toward the face
that laves me with ravelling
water of crystalline fineness.
                 The wine of your own loveliness
                 spins your head. No
keep away from the others,
their sodden debauch.
                 Promise promise even a lie
                 & I will believe you;
try, kiss yourself, taste
from your own lips the Water of Life.
                 Dust at your feet I wait
                 the last drops spilled from your cup;
subtle so subtle I know
you are my own soul.
                 One moment manifest, one hidden
                 to my eyes, my heart, your gentleness;
your words drip as
pearls into my ears. . .
                 Sweet child, Iraqi chokes without
                 the life of your mouth.

III. A Commentary

The world of Persian poetry has this peculiarity: it is
founded in a "Hyperborean," Aryan and Mazdaean past,

and transformed by Islam. In this sense it resembles the Japanese world, founded in Shinto and transformed by the Chinese tradition and again by Buddhism. Such a collision of world-views is like a marriage; indeed, it is often symbolized in a myth of the mating of divinities of the two peoples who have collided. The original and "pure" Persian world is now almost totally lost; we know it largely through the creations of Islamic poets like Ferdowsi. But the energies released by the collision were terrific: within a few centuries of the Arab invasion a flood of literature began to pour forth. I don't intend to try to separate the Islamic and pre-Islamic currents within this body of poetry, but rather to investigate the way in which its reservoir of imagery was used by certain poets.

A body of imagery related to the archetypes can of course be used for "profane" purposes. But by the very fact of its archetypal connections it can always reverse its polarity and refer back to "sacred" origins. Thus the drinking songs of Rudaki and the panegyrics of the early Persian court poets use the same traditional imagery as the early sufi poets such as Sana'i. Certain great writers such as Shakespeare or Hafez consciously play with this ambiguous or two-faced quality of symbolism.

A symbol like Wine gains in power for the Persian poet precisely because Islam forbids it, yet promises it to the faithful in paradise. In this as in many other instances Islam draws a hard clear line between the Outer and Inner, between symbol and significance. To play with this line, to break it with words, produces a shock which is both aesthetic and spiritual.

"Forget the Kaaba—the vintner's gates are open," says Iraqi; in other words, forget the pilgrimage to Mecca, one of Islam's central rites, and make your way to the tavern to consort with drunkards. What Iraqi means is that the spiritual intoxication to be gained by associating with sufis takes priority over the outward duties pre-scribed by Law. But the words of the poem, considered simply as an image, are shocking. To explain away such images by a series of mathematical equations ("wine" = "spiritual intoxication," "tavern" = "sufi meeting house," etc.) cannot do justice to the intentional ambiguity of a poet like Iraqi. The juxtaposition of "sacred" and "profane" or Islamic and non-Islamic imagery constitutes a kind of Scylla and Charybdis between which the reader must slip, with the speed of a paradox or the trans-logic of a pun. On the other side of such an image, all ambiguity is resolved, all symbols penetrated, all seeming contradictions transcended. A landscape which at first appeared fraught with danger is now suffused with golden light. The reader has been given neither a simple drinking song nor a pious hymn, but a riddle, and the answer shocks him awake. The poet uses symbolism to reach the archetypes, to pass beyond into the spiritual "state" *(hal)* of the metaphysical experience, the Unity of Being.

The way in which a poem is made does not lend itself to simple schematization—but let us pretend for a moment, and separate into various stages that process which by its very nature escapes the linear quality of ordinary mentation. Let us assume that the sufi poet begins with a moment of pure intuition—the metaphysical experience of the Unity of Being—which takes place on the level of the Heart (Spirit or *nous*). Because he is a poet, this intuition at once begins to resolve itself into images of an archetypal nature. His soul, like an alchemical apparatus, distills these images into rhythms and words. By the exercise of reason and craft, the words are organized into a poem.

(Of course the poet can "begin" with any one of these stages, or with all at once. The scheme presented here is not necessarily a temporal sequence but rather an onto-logical/epistemological hierarchy.)

The purpose of this activity is two-fold: first, to crystallize for the poet his own contemplative intuition— this is part of the process of his own Self-integration or "realization," as necessary to him, as an individual, as is prayer to the worshipper or the act of love to the lover. Second, to transmit this intuition to someone else—for that is the duty imposed on him by the Muse.

The poem thus serves the illumination of both the poet and his audience. It emerges out of contemplation and is filtered (like light through stained glass) through the imagery of the poet's traditional world, the world he is given; and through the imagery of his own psyche, the world he gives. Both levels of imagery relate to the archetypes, but in different ways. The success of the poet depends on how well he integrates the two levels; in other words, how completely he lives the archetypal imagery, how totally he Imagines it, makes it is his own and re-creates it both for himself and his audience.

If the sufi poet has succeeded in this task, the poem itself can now be contemplated by the audience. The listener will be drawn back toward the "state" the poet wished to evoke, in a reversal of the creative process outlined above. (Needless to say, much of this schematization can relate to any "spiritual" poet, not just a Persian sufi poet. But the latter is a special case because he is so conscious of this particular poetic purpose, and so successful within his cultural context—as I shall try to show.)

As an object of contemplation—or at least as a support for contemplation—the poem plays the role of an icon. The metaphor is a bit loose, of course, because the painted icon is part of an actual ritual, and is produced according to strict canons to serve a liturgical purpose; while the sufi poem is produced outside the liturgical context of Islam. The sufi poem follows certain traditional patterns, but is not canonically regulated.

However, the metaphor can be justified on other grounds. In the first place, although Islam does not "forbid" the painted image, it certainly hesitates to accord the representational arts any central place in its universe. In

T. Burckhardt's phrase, Islam is not inherently iconoclastic, but rather "aniconic". Above all, it is a religion "of the Book", of the Word. Thus, in the context of Islamic culture, Imaginal energies tend to be concentrated much more in the arts of the word than in the representational arts. Calligraphy and poetry bear more of the burden of the Imagination in Islamic than in Christian or Buddhist art; they are more "central".

In the second place, sufism has developed its own extra-liturgical forms of ritual. These center around the practise of *zekr,* invocation of the divine Names, "quintessential prayer". *Zekr* is required of all Moslems, but only in the general sense of "remembrance"; (as in the Koranic injunction, "Remember Me (God), I will remember you"). Usually, only the sufis have regularized it and ritualized it. Ceremonies of *zekr* are enriched by other activities, including the recitation of certain prayers and formulae, and in some Orders the performance of music and poetry.

❁   ❁   ❁

Before dealing with this quasi-liturgical use of poetry, however, let us explore some of the ways in which sufi poets make use of what might be called iconic imagery. Obviously we cannot attempt an over-all view of sufi imagery, so we will concentrate on a single poem, one of the short lyrics by Fakhroddin Iraqi given in the last section of this chapter.

Poems of this type (the *ghazal*) often appear much less organized or unified than short lyrics in English. They are composed in couplets, and each couplet may represent a single image or thought. A *ghazal* is unified by meter and rhyme but not necessarily by a strong central theme; the couplets are "pearls loosely strung." Sometimes however the *ghazal* is more tightly organized, building up couplet by couplet into a unified field of imagery, a single "icon", even though perhaps lacking a single focus. Iraqi's poem is of this type. It is woven into just such an Imaginal scene. It presents an invitation to the reader to leave his home and come to the tavern, and to walk with his beloved in a beautiful garden. It then offers a description of these pleasures, and ends with a re-iteration of the invitation in more openly gnostic terms.

> The tavern doors swing wide;
> Drink, my heart: wine unravels all knots.
>> Stare not at yourself but
>> in the idol's flower-lidded eyes.
> Forget the Kaaba:
> the vintner's gates are open;
>> come out, see the beloved's face,
>> leave the house: the garden is unlocked. . . .

No better source for an explanation of these images exists than Mahmud Shabestari's *Gulshan-i raz,* the *Rosegarden of Mystery,* a poem of 1007 lines explaining virtually all of sufism (from the point of view of the Persian School of Ibn Arabi, to which Iraqi also belonged) in terms of literary symbolism.

As for the tavern, on one level it is the spiritual world itself, the realm of the Imagination intoxicated by the vision of divine Love. In fact, it transcends the Imagination and approximates more nearly to the level of the Intuitive Intellect which undergoes direct metaphysical experience without recourse to images:

> The tavern is of the world that has no similitude
> [i.e., that outreaches the dualism of symbol and significance].
>> The tavern is the nest of the bird of the soul,
>> the tavern is the sanctuary that has no place.

Iraqi says that the tavern doors are open; usually

they are occulted, closed (Hafez says that even the angels of heaven must knock at the tavern door)—so if they are open, a magical moment is at hand, an opportunity to acquire some spiritual treasure.

Wine is the treasure. Shabestari urges us to seize the moment:

> Drink wine that it may set you free from yourself. . .
> Drink wine, for its cup is the face of the Friend

[i.e., the face of God is reflected in the cup of wine, which thus represents the locus of theophany, the experience of the divine in created things].

> The cup is His eye drunken and flown with wine.
> Seek wine without cup or goblet

[i.e., beyond all manifestation]. . .

> Pure wine is that which gives you purification
>   from the stain of existence at the time of
>   intoxication. . .
> The whole universe is as His winehouse,
>   the heart of every atom as His winecup.
> Reason is drunken, angels drunken, soul drunken,
>   air drunken, earth drunken, heaven drunken.

The idol again refers to the manifestation of the divine in created things; sometimes it refers to an actual religious statue, more often to a beautiful girl or boy. Shabestari says:

> Idol-worship is essentially Unification.
> Since all things are manifestors of Being,
> one amongst them must be an idol.
> Consider well, O wise man,
> an idol as regards its real being is not vain. . .
> If the Moslem but knew what is faith,
> he would see that faith is idol-worship.

God, say the sufis, cannot be "known" in His unqualified Essence, but only in the forms He assumes (what the Hindus call the dance of Shiva). On another level, this "idol-worship" justifies the spiritual technique of the icon, the visual or sensible support for contemplation.

To elucidate the image of the Beloved would require an explanation of all sufism in terms of Love, which is beyond our scope. Suffice it to hint: God created man "in His own image", and the human form is the most perfect manifestation of the divine. The Beloved of sufi poetry does not simply "stand for" or allegorize a transcendent deity. The loved one may be simultaneously a human beloved and the locus of manifestation of divine Beauty— as was Beatrice for Dante. This highest sense of the science of symbolism must be kept in mind if the ambiguity of a poem like that of Iraqi's is to be penetrated.

If this be the case, then each of the Beloved's features reveals some divine mystery. For Iraqi, for example, the tress or curl seems to signify that which the Hindus call *Maya:* illusion to the unititiated, but revelation to the one who knows. Shabestari says:

> If He shakes aside those black curls of His
> no single infidel is left in the world.
> If He leaves them continually in their place,
> there remains not in the world one faithful soul.
> That spider's web of His is spread as a net to
>   ensnare,
> in wantonness He puts it aside from off His
>   face. . .
> That curl is never at rest for a moment,
> now it brings morning and now evening.
> With His face and curl He makes day and night,
> sporting with them in marvellous fashion.

This sport is the divine play *(lila)* of Hinduism. *Deus ludens* appears wanton and arbitrary, now offering union, now separation—just like a capricious girl or boy.

As for the garden: Nature too is a perfect manifestation of divine Beauty, and the garden is quintessential Nature, the earthly paradise *(pardes, firdaus, hortus conclusus)*. The garden is Nature transformed by symbolic vision, and by the direct perception of God's "Mercy", His creative beneficence. Thus it serves as the perfect background for the poem (equivalent to the gold-leaf of an icon—"a spring of light pours on the earth's eyes"). Shabestari calls his own poem a Rose-garden: from it

> I have plucked this bouquet
> which I have named the Rose-garden of mystery.
> Therein the roses of hearts' mystery are blooming,
> whereof none has told heretofore.
> Therein the tongues of the lilies are all vocal,
> the eyes of the narcissus are all far-seeing.
> Regard each one with the eye of the Heart.

Here is the key to the understanding of the poem as icon: the images are like flowers which must be seen with "the eye of the Heart", symbols which must be penetrated with the active Imagination. Only then will their messages be sensed—only then will the images speak and unveil their mysteries.

If, like Iraqi, we close our doors (by shutting off our "profane" senses through contemplation) the Friend's door will open: the "Unveiling of the Mysteries". Only then will the world become for us a treasury, or rather an icon which holds the key to metaphysical experience.

But how can a poem achieve this? Are not poems but collections of words, and are not words mere arbitrary signs, alphabetic conventions which cannot in themselves provide a means of penetrating to the reality behind them? Not according to Shabestari. In speaking of certain key terms (such as we've been discussing) he writes

> When these words are heard by the sensual ear,

at first they denote objects of sense.
The spiritual world is infinite;
how can finite words attain to it?
How can the mysteries beheld in ecstatic vision
be interpreted by spoken words?
When mystics treat of these mysteries
they interpret them by types.
For objects of sense are as shadows of that world,
and this world is as an infant, and that as the
    nurse.
I believe that these words were at first assigned
to those mysteries in their original usage.
They were afterwards assigned to objects of sense
by usage of the vulgar
(for what do the vulgar know of these mysteries?)
And when reason turned its glance on the world,
it transferred some words from that place
[i.e., from spiritual objects to sensible objects].

Words, if thus properly understood, are like dispersed rays of the primordial Logos, the Word which brought Being into manifestation. The duty of the poet as icon-maker is to use these words in such a way as to refocus the rays into a complex of imagery which points back, through the Logos, to the true Source of Being.

❁   ❁   ❁

In Persia the "bardic age" has survived, in part, longer than in the West. Some years ago I was walking home late one winter night through a new section of Tehran devoted to badly-built imitation sky-scapers. In the steel rib-cage of a tower still under construction, a night watchman had built himself a fire of broken boxes. Huddled in a long sheepskin coat, he was chanting poetry to himself; Hafez, I think.

Despite the vicissitudes of recent history the Iranian

soul still harbors a love of poetry and music; and even (or perhaps especially) the illiterate memorize thousands of verses of Firdawsi and Rumi. But to call Persia "bardic" does not merely imply a sentimental attachment to the arts on the part of peasant or traditional literatus.

The twelve modes of classical Persian music, which some scholars link to the signs of the Zodiac or the Zoroastrian angels of the months, have preserved integral links with the meters of classical poetry. This means that any poem written in such a meter can be performed, either as a simple unaccompanied chant, or in a more sophisticated style of singing accompanied by traditional instruments. As Nora Chadwick points out in *Poetry and Prophecy,* this combination of words and music is the archetypal language of the spiritual world, the means by which shaman or bard links the ordinary consciousness of his audience to the elevated consciousness of higher "non-ordinary" states. It is rather as if the techniques of the author of Beowulf had survived and been refined, so that even today an English or American poet possessed the option of a traditional but still vital oral/aural mode of presentation.

This "language of the birds", this potent survival of an archaic form of poetic expression, constitutes a precious treasure of Persian art, and the means whereby the written poem may be animated and transformed into an "icon".

The extra-liturgical ceremonies of the sufi Orders make use of poetry and music in the rite known as *sama'*, "audition". Some Orders emphasize strongly rhythmic music and dance, while others prefer subtler rhythms and mystical poetry. In the mainstream Persian Orders, the *majlis* or meeting often begins with the chanting of poetry by a talented dervish. The Khaksariyya make use of Hafez, whom they claim as one of their spiritual ancestors. I have already mentioned a session in Shiraz, where the Order possesses a beautiful garden near the tomb of

Hafez; it was an extraordinary experience to witness the continuing power of Shiraz's favorite poet over Shiraz's mystics.

The Nematollahi Order naturally favors the *Divan* of their founder, Shah Nematollah Vali (who is also very popular with the Ismailis of Khorassan and Badakhshan) and their later masters such as Nur Ali Shah. The present *Qutb* or head of the Order, Javad Nurbakhsh, has also produced a small *Divan* which is much performed. Amongst the Ahl-i Haqq ("People of Truth"), a sufi-influenced sect originating in Kurdestan, Rumi's *Divan-i Shams* is a favorite source. One recent master of the Ahl-i Haqq, Ustad Ilahi, was himself a brilliant musician, and attracted some of the finest young classical performers to his *jam'-khaneh* or meeting-house in Tehran. While the mainstream sufi Orders generally eschew instrumentation (due to the memory of the severe persecution of the Orders by the exoteric authorities in the Nineteenth century), the Ahl-i Haqq play a stringed instrument called the tambour.

"Audition" has a wonderful effect on the dervishes. Even the uneducated among them are familiar with the symbolism and intellectual purport of the poetry, or indeed know many of the poems by heart. Listening to brilliant and emotional performances in the closed circle of an entirely sympathetic audience, they abandon themselves with fervor to the magic spell of the poetry; they weep, they sway with the rhythm, they cry out in ecstasy at the particularly pointed resolution of a flow of imagery. Through the *sama'* they have attained a *hal* or spiritual state which plunges them into the invocation, sometimes accompanied by spontaneous or ritualized dance.

Now in the mystic dance of joy in the Beloved,
losing head and foot like the revolving heavens,
in every strain they hear from the minstrel
comes to them rapture from the unseen world.

✱ 150 *✱*

The mystic song is not those mere words and
    sounds,
for in every note thereof lies a precious mystery.

(Shabestari)

Plate 1. "Lingayat Saddhus and Nematollahi Dervishes" (see page 20-24).

Plate 2. **"The Weeping Eye"** (see page 165).

Plate 3. "**Al-Buraq an-Nabī**" [Winged Woman-Mule] (see page 174).

Plate 4. **"Semar as Allah"** [Green and gold painting on glass] (see pages 183-93).

Plates 5a-5e. **"Semar"** (see pages 183-93):

5a. **"Semar"** [From a pamphlet on Wayang].

5b. **"Semar as Allah"**.

5c. **"Semar as Allah"**.

5d. **"Semar as Allah"**.

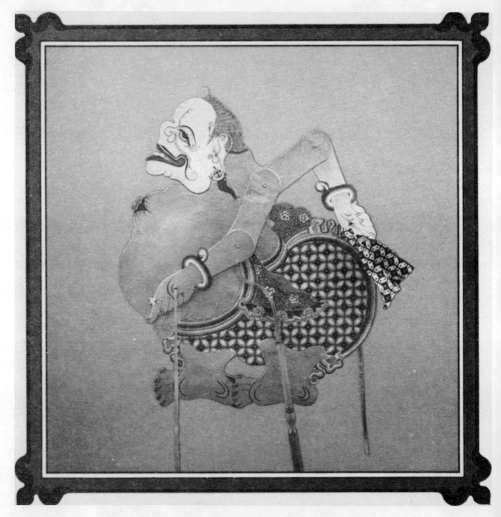

5e. **"Semar"** [Javanese greeting-card].

Plate 6. **"Whirling Dervish"** [Author's photo] (see page 200).

Plate 7. **"Greeting Cards"** [Two Islamic 'Id greeting cards, one depicting the Kaaba, the other in "pop-up" format] (see pages 153-57).

Plate 8. **"Calligraphic Face"** [According to the *Hurufiyya*, or the "Abecedarians," both Macrocosm and Microcosm (i.e., humanity) can be expressed in the forms of the sacred Arabic alphabet. The *Hurufiyya* were eliminated as heretics but their teaching has influenced much Turkish popular religious art, especially the "calligramme"] (see pages 164-66).

Plate 9. **"Mantra Ghaib"** [Cover of a popular pamphlet on sorcery published in Java, "Secret Incantations"] (see page 159).

Plate 10. **"Noble Drew Ali"** (see pages 28-30).

Plate 11. **"The Hand of Ali"** [A woodblock print on rice paper used as an amulet, and showing various symbols associated with Ali ibn Abi Taleb, the Prophet's son-in-law, founder of both Shi'ism and sufism] (see pages 164-66).

6

Ambiguous Icons:
Representational & Popular Religious Art in Islam

1. Low Taste

At the tribal level no art is "religious" since no concept of religion per se yet exists, and art is still an integral part of a total way of life penetrated more or less completely by spirit. With the emergence of civilization art and religion become categories. Official religious art emerges, the canonical and orthodox production of an institutionalized cult.

But aside from (or underneath) this official art, each civilized culture contains another form of spiritual art which is not official and canonical. It is produced, anonymously and often commercially, to satisfy ritual and spiritual needs which are not or cannot be satisfied by the established cult.

This art could hardly be called marginal, since it is used by vast numbers of people (i.e., it is "popular")—but it has been ignored by art history because of its vernacular values, its ephemeral nature, and its ambiguous relation with "official" concepts of both art and history.

Popular religious art may be "low" compared to "high" classical religious art—but this is a matter of style rather than of value judgement, for the most part. An excellent piece of popular religious art can fulfil all the purposes of spiritual art with as much success—in its way—as does a piece of high-classical art in its way. More: the popular piece, if it is made with clear vision and taste, far exceeds in value a classical piece made by dull rote, lacking any spark of immediacy. After all, spiritual art is for something; it is for waking up our sleeping ordinary second-or-third-rate consciousness. Often a naive piece can accomplish this better than a "fine" one; this is an aesthetic value understood by the Japanese tea-men. The naive artist can exemplify what in Zen is called "beginner's mind": child-like, but somehow also perfectly realized.

Is a great and truly-inspired piece of classical art "better than" anything—however excellent—in the "low" or popular category? In some senses undoubtedly. But there is more to be gained by appreciating a good piece on its own merits than by slotting it into a hierarchy. The authentic is always moving, whatever its style; and its style is a sign of its authenticity. Both high and low can fall prey to ennervating formalism. Popular art can be trivialized, vulgarized. Classical art can decline through a stuffy rigidity, a stiffening of the blood. However it is not failure but success which defines an artistic category. A cheap colored print, the impress of Garuda on a bottle of soda-water, a crudely-printed yantra. . .sometimes these images are so well-realized by their designs that they seem to fill up the entire aesthetic space for which they were intended, leaving no room for comparison. Their efficacy is not limited by their reproduction nor reduced by their simplicity. They work.

Spiritual imagery used to sell a product, or even treated as a product in itself, may be in one sense trivialized, but in another sense it may serve to inject even the world of banal multiplicity with magic. To see Ganesha on a packet of Indian cigarettes is to be reminded of the sacredness of beginnings; to see a Taoist Immortal on a packet of incense is to be reminded of infinitude and the wisdom of the senses. Certain styles of Chinese and Japanese calligraphy are so tense with accumulated awareness that their effect in neon signs can be overpowering.

The choice of very "low" examples is deliberate. If one were to speak instead of unique artifacts like ex-votos or Yao Taoist paintings or Palach icons, the argument for the power of popular religious art would be easier to make. But this would not negate the fact that spiritual beauty constantly hungers to be realized, and may blossom on a medicine label as easily as in a temple. The popular artist works most often with the same "vocabulary" as the classical artist; indeed, classical art often hands down this image-horde to popular art. But the popular artist, by the exuberance and directness with which he uses the elements of the tradition, gives something back to the whole of that tradition, a vitality which renews high and low alike.

Modern technology has a way of wiping out traditional aesthetics. It seems to erode the sense of style. Since the nineteenth century a number of traditional civilizations have been more or less suddenly penetrated by a technology radically more "advanced" than their own. The social ecology and aesthetic fabric of an ancient city can be ruined by the rapidity of internal combustion; and something similar can happen to artistic and spiritual taste. However, the sense of beauty which belongs to a collectivity cannot be wiped out overnight and totally. Ancient civilizations undergoing this sort of "invasion" experience a period of transition, when only a few modern tools have yet been accepted, and in which the new technology actually produces a new kind of vitality. For example, sewing machines are used to manufacture traditional embroideries, or printing is used to disseminate spiritual imagery. In the nineteenth century a number of westernized Persians in Tehran ordered huge gilt-framed mirrors from France. Unloaded from ships in the Persian Gulf and transported by camel caravan over the Zagros mountains, many of them broke. The shards were sold cheaply to traditional mosaic tile workers, who cut them into regular shapes and used them—along with stained glass—to decorate the insides and outsides of religious buildings and even the homes of the well-to-do. The result was a brief flowering of an exotic and potent style, a prismatic fantasia in which the sun plays a central role in the creation of experienced architectural space. The observer enters into the heart of Light; the effect is overpowering, psychedelic. . .vulgar perhaps, but alive and exciting.

After such a transitional period, modern technology tends to get the upper hand. A small tribe is quickly engulfed, while a great civilization like Indian or China can probably never fully collapse. But the end results of high technology for traditional spiritual art do not appear to be beneficial.

Some countries are, at this very moment, undergoing typical transitional periods, and thus producing popular religious art of great interest. In fully modernized countries artists sometimes come full circle to a new appreciation of traditional spiritual forms and try to adapt aspects of traditional art to their own particular needs. In such projects, tribal, folk, naive and popular art often prove even more useful than classical art. Immediacy and intensity seem sometimes to work better than austerity and iconic rigidity. Paradoxically and sadly, eyes often open to the beauty of such art just as it is in danger of vanishing forever. It cannot be artificially sustained by UNESCO grants or National Folk Ensembles. Popular culture does not pickle well. Either it is popular or it is dead.

2. No Ideas But In Things

Whatever is human must also be sacred. A little reading in anthropology will demonstrate that everything—every object and every deed—has at some time in some culture been religiously celebrated or endowed with the quality of *mana* or *baraka*. "Chopping wood and drawing water": the simplest of actions and the most basic substances already represent everything a spiritual path has to offer, simply in their quality of being. People seek—on various levels of consciousness—to remind themselves of this by a ritualization of everyday life. On the tribal level the face between ritual and life is often so blurred as to be unrecognizable. In civilized cultures greater division is felt between sacred and profane.

The danger in such ritualization is superstition: being possessed by images rather than freed by them. Even in "low" art, the images themselves however very often seem the products of genuine vision. The art-objects are fully adequate vehicles for spiritual realization. The fact that they may be copied or even mass-produced, or that their style is "anonymous" or even crude, cannot detract from the quality of the initial vision and creative impulse which brought them into being. Nor are they lessened by their localness, by the vocabulary supplied by environment, tradition, class and condition.

The image of a deity, angel or mythological being may serve as a focus for prayer or meditation, or it may simply be considered "auspicious" and used on a patent-medicine label. Certain civilizations—especially the polytheistic ones—seem to live under a cornucopia of Imaginal imagery which spills out a sea of visions, a continual penetration of life by dream, of thought by imagination. Even Islam has its popular icons—moon, minaret, rose, Kaaba and Buraq—which gain in intensity by their endless and musical repetition. Each civilization, culture, people, profession, family and individual lives under certain signs, by which they know and are known.

The negative aspects of existence are just as much part of everyday life—and of the Imagination—as the positive ones. To ritualize pain, suffering and disruptive emotion is partly to mitigate them and partly to master them. By knowing the sign of a demon, its image, one may be able to escape its malignancy; by knowing it for an aspect of the self, one may be able to reverse its polarity and turn its power to one's own positive use.

Tibetans, Indonesians, Taoists and tantriks "convert" the most horrific images they can spin up into the very guardians of their spiritual welfare, just as the Prophet is said to have converted the djinn to Islam. In less esoteric climates, with more rigid notions of good and evil, these monsters are forced underground, sometimes to an official Hell and sometimes right down to the bedrock of the unconscious mind, that sink of demonolatry. But no culture exists without some ritualization of these dark forces.

Eros is also disruptive, and no culture has ever lacked some means of ordering and channeling it. The individual however cannot but feel the liberating aspects of its energy. In some place or tribe or culture at some time or another, every imaginable erotic and romantic mode has been condoned and even thought spiritually important— including all sorts of reversals of ordinary sexuality. Eros is the sign of the doubleness of the individual's relation to society. A source of conflict can be a source of power, and indeed much creativity (as well as much oppression) flows out of the contemplation of our desires.

Islam combines rigorous puritanism in its outer (*zaher*) aspect with an intensely erotic inner (*baten*) reality. The

Prophet approved of sexual pleasure, and said that "Three things of this world I love: perfume, women and prayer, in which is the coolness of my eyes." Ibn Arabi devoted a chapter of *Bezels of Wisdom* to elucidating a sort of "sufi tantra", a total spiritualization of Eros. The Koran's images of paradise as a garden of houris, cupbearers and wine provide an erotic basis for all Islamic culture. Popular religious art in Islam deals obsessively with images of romance and desire.

At its best such art possesses a magic quality which by-passes aesthetic judgement. And in truth much of this art is meant to serve magical purposes. He who controls the archetypes that govern man and nature thereby controls man and nature. In popular culture, magic and its imagery often shade off into mere superstition, especially in the obsession with "bad luck", greed and hostility. One does not have to believe in the supernatural to accept that black magic, like advertising, sometimes works.

A certain kind of adept will point out that the true miracle is existence itself. Magic, whether it works or not, is rather beside the point. But if popular magic shades downwards into superstition it also shades upwards into the way of the adept. For mystics who are not drawn to (or are denied) high/classical/spiritual/religious techniques, magic offers a path which is open and full of color. High initiates of magic know that the final purpose of their rites is union with the deity and the acquisition of the knowledge of the gods. This world is a reflection of their world and they cast their mirror images on earth when they possess or appear to their worshippers. Human intercourse with them is beneficial, inasmuch as it makes clear the way in which the mandalas of earth and heaven are identified.

In one sense mysticism transcends all imagery and therefore all art. This is well known and it is no use repeating all the arguments about "Truth" not being found in books (or pictures). But it is easy to lose sight of the fact that from another point of view the mystic does not transcend imagery at all. Being-in-itself is unknowable; all that we know we know through forms; therefore what the mystic knows he knows through form and image ("and this," as Ibn Arabi says, "is the vision of God in created things, which, in the opinion of some, is higher than the vision of created things in God"). The mystic does not know Being-in-itself because "in that state, there is neither knower nor known." To the extent the mystic remains an individual he retains contact with form and image. Indeed, he may be said to occupy the same place from which all form and image flow, the nexus of Being and multiplicity; and in this Orphic sense the mystic and artist are one.

Any image can provide some necessary clue to self-realization. It depends at least as much on who is seeing the image as on the image itself. Each individual has an individual archetype, personal guardian angel, ruling divine aspect or *ishta devata* (*rabb,* or "Lord", as Ibn Arabi called it). Moreover, each individual has a constellation of archetypes, forms and images which concern him, which are part of the soul, collected from a myriad sources, some shared with others, some dark and lonely—and each set as different as fingerprints or the whorls of the ear or patterns of the retina.

For the traditional artist much of the imagery he uses will be supplied by tradition. And if he lives that tradition and interiorizes it, he renews it. But always, even in the most strict orthodox canons, something must be left specifically to the individual. For the popular artist, less restricted by the rules of the temple, the personal element is magnified, despite—or perhaps because of—his very anonymity.

This discussion of popular religious art can only provide a loose framework for thinking in a given moment, set of circumstances and mode of perception. This particular framework is based on an attempt to experience the phenomena from within rather than from outside them. That is to say, in order to study popular religious art one must know the point of view which produced that art; and one must share it, at least operationally and by accepting it as valid within the terms proposed. Little is to be gained by bringing alien criteria (be they aesthetic, political, religious or scientific) to bear on cultural or artistic phenomena which already possess in themselves coherent self-explanations and fully-realized structures. In order to learn, one listens and watches, making use of knowledge acquired from other sources but always respectful of the special skill or knowledge being displayed. This may sound obvious or even banal, but until very recently it has not been widely accepted as a valid mode of operation for studying other cultures or comparing them with each other and with our own. First Christianity and then imperialism and other political or religious ideologies have dictated the way in which we have observed and experienced "foreign" cultures: mostly as sources of plunder and as mires of ignorance.

However tentatively, we can now approach popular religious art on its own terms, using categories which would be acceptable to the cultures under discussion, and yet at the same time able to provide conceptual bridges from culture to culture.

3. Forbidden Images

Islam is said to be an iconoclastic religion. The overwhelming majority of the classical Islamic visual arts exhibit an adherence to non-representationalism, to an abstract ideal; not in the sense of modern Western art, which abstracts from representation toward some ideal form, but rather in the sense that Islamic art *begins* with abstract forms, crystalline and organic, and produces from them a repetitive but more than merely decorative art and architecture. The general absence of representation in these arts reinforces the impression of Islam's anti-imagism. The Faith appears as a vast and precise geometry of light and space, mantric and mandalic, molecular and mathematical, serene and empty of distraction, an ordering of perception into spiritual growth.

Even the miniature book-illustrations of Persia and India fit into this over-all pattern, since they make use of geometric compositions of lucid color rather than perspective and chiaroscuro, and are almost always pictures of narrative rather than of single observed moments. (This holds perfectly true only for early miniatures, and not always for later artists or spontaneous geniuses like the Turk Kalam Siyah, or Reza Abbasi of Isfahan; nor for the later Moghul miniaturists. Perspective however never enters Islamic art without destroying or at least severely compromising its basic essence.)

In effect, as T. Burckhardt has said, Islam is not iconoclastic but aniconic—if not in the strictly jurisprudential sense, then certainly in its main cultural flowering. The "peace" which Islam seeks in its arts arises not from hatred of the image, but rather from an alchemical spiritualization or sublimation of the senses. All Islamic art implies an Image, but one that cannot be openly stated: the Image of the One. Islamic art asks us to use our Imagination in an active relation between art-object and viewer, to allow the object to evoke our own creative apperception of Oneness.

This much is true. But Islam has also acted historically and jurisprudentially as an iconoclastic force. Not only great non-Islamic art has been destroyed, but also art produced by Moslems. The punishments meted out in Gehenna to iconodules and artists are all quite clear, even in the hadith of the Prophet himself. Fanatics like the Moghul emperor Aurangzeb or the puritanical Wahhabis of Saudi Arabia would utterly condemn all representational art if they could. Not even a mirror is allowed in any mosque, anywhere in the Islamic world, not even by the wildest Shiite.

But—again—despite this severity, the Islamic cultures of Persia, India and Java (for examples) have produced and still produce vast amounts of representational art. Classical miniatures have been overvalued by Western art historians, who are biased against "mere decoration" (a category into which they dump all the truly central Islamic arts, such as calligraphy). But other kinds of representational art have been totally ignored by the pundits, either because they find it "popular" and vulgar, not really ART at all; or because, since it is representational, it cannot really be Islamic art. This neat solution however fails to make the artifacts in question disappear.

In order to deal with this confusion, we might make use of a scheme or chart of definitions. We might say that Islamic art can be divided into categories, thus:

(1) Canonical art. Used in mosques and on liturgical objects. It cannot be called "sacred art" in the strict sense, since no one adores it as Christians adore icons of the Messiah, or Buddhists of the Buddha. But it obeys Koranic and Traditional strictures and limits itself to the "abstract".

(2) Classical art. Imitates canonical art in secular settings, thus lending a generally-diffused "sacredness" to Islamic culture. But it need not be limited by liturgical considerations, and therefore allows representation under certain conditions—as with Persian miniatures for example.

(3) Popular art. A primarily non-imagistic culture such as Islam cannot satisfy every human need for visual stimulation, it seems. Nor can every converted non-Arab people adapt to even the most relaxed and tolerant of aniconic atmospheres. Imagery must spring up and flower almost everywhere. In the Islamic world this impulse cannot always be gratified by the Canonical and Classical arts. Therefore a truly popular art arises as the expression of a spiritual collective consciousness; and also as a

means of self-expression for artists who do not fit within traditional or Legal bounds. It can thus be extremely conservative, in that it might look back to pre-Islamic figurative forms; and it can also be "radical" in that it opposes or stands outside strict orthodoxy. Sometimes it can be both, simultaneously.

The inner history of Islamic art discloses itself in a development toward perfect taste.

The word "taste" must not be taken in the usual sense of "personal preference" and/or "sophistication". Above all, taste is *zawq*, "spiritual taste". To experience and absorb something to its core and essence bestows Certainty. In a poem, a pattern of tiles or a carved begging bowl, the *ahl-i zawq* or people of taste will discern the presence or absence of spiritual discernment as well as artistic skill.

The Islamic obsession with Unity (*tawhid*) drives artistic taste in a certain direction: toward patterns that embody the almost numerological metaphysics of Unity-in-multiplicity, open-ended patterns within closed patterns. An illuminated Koran page is a section cut out of an eternally-repeated geometry of light.

Repetition of a "true" pattern, one of the grid-structures underlying the very fabric of reality, becomes for Moslem taste analogous to the repetition of a divine Name. The element of subjectivity is purposefully eliminated till all that remains is a single moment of aesthetic/spiritual perception, the mirror-reflection of a heart that has chosen the Real.

Calligraphy and pattern, which the West calls "minor arts", are in fact the quintessence and apotheosis of Islamic culture. A serenity which is noble, a beauty which is sublimed of all history, all egotism: these represent the highest aesthetic for the Classical periods (Fatimid, Seljuk, Ommayad, etc.) and a constantly recurring flavor even in the later flowerings of Timurid, Mughal, Safavid, Ottoman, Andalusian-Moorish. That which is impersonal can become "rich" to the point of Safavid ultra-refinement or "poor" as the mud-mosques of Africa, without losing that harmony of taste and nostalgia for pure light which inform the most virile and archaic periods of mainstream Islamic art. Always, even in the most baroque and decadent periods, the presence of the sword can be felt, however hidden, however subtle: a blade that reduces all complexity to the simple, all desire to fulfilment, all color to light. If this spirit is lost the art becomes at once noticeably non-Islamic, no matter what its subject matter.

The popular religious art reproduced in this book offends against the canons of Islamic taste in many ways. By Classical standards some of it is decadent to the point of kitsch—or at least a purist might say so. Certainly no one would defend these examples as High Art of any sort. Having admitted all that, I must also admit to a bias. I find these pieces delightful and beautiful. It is not an acquired taste, but an intuitive and immediate response. This art awakens me, and I have tried to understand why.

At its most austere, Islamic art can come to seem almost devoid of the spirit of play. But these popular pieces have an unexpected quality, in some cases a bizarre day-dreaminess, that recalls childish playfulness and the fresh vision of the naive artist. Play does not imply lack of seriousness. All these examples are religious in intent; but each is touched with a hint of improvisation, the sense of discovery. Some are openly emotional in a way that Classical Islamic art generally eschews, but they escape mere sentimentality. In "The Weeping Eye" (Pl. 2) for example, the crude emotionalism of the central image is muted, refined and abstracted by the coolness of the calligraphy. The sword of Unity is there somewhere, despite the Art-Deco taste. The very lightness of such a work, its lack of all ponderous royal and ecclesial "richness", its spontaneous imagination and lack of polish: these qualities override any lapses of taste.

Moreover, each of the works chosen here remains

Islamic in the deepest sense, despite the fact that some of them were produced by heretics and schismatics. A pratising Moslem might conceivably paint a picture in a purely Western style, or a purely Japanese style for that matter, but it would not be an Islamic painting. My popular works may lie well outside any main current of Islamic culture, and in some cases may deal with material that many Moslems would find offensive. But none of these examples use perpective or conventional realism. All of them seek inspiration from the basic sources of Word and Pattern. All of them use symbolism in a traditional way. All avoid any egotistical or subjective statements. All are concerned with spiritual values.

Although none of the artists have vaunted their egos, some of them have succeeded in expressing a uniqueness or "personness" which sometimes cannot be found in Classical Islamic art. Canons and traditions ensure the perpetuation of taste, but may not allow for personal and untutored genius to blossom. Perfection of surface can threaten to drive out authenticity of vision. Endless repetition of beauty can veer toward stasis. These minor popular eruptions of spontaneity do not betray the tradition but may actually help to "make it new", as Confucius is supposed to have said. In fact in a world where much of Islamic art is dead these twentieth century examples represent a continuity of tradition, not its demise.

In a book we are limited to looking at flat pictures, but an even better example of popular religious art in Islam is the Persian "Passion Play" or *ta'zieh*. It grew out of ritual Ashura processions commemorating the martyrdom of Husayn, grandson of the Prophet and Imam of the Shiites. Increasingly complex parades finally ground to a halt sometime in the eighteenth century and became theater-pieces. (Indian Shiites retain the earlier form of elaborate marches of penitenti and symbolic "floats".) Music, costume, declamation and chanting of dramatic verse, props, live animals, eventually even theater buildings designed expressly for *ta'zieh:* all this is in effect quite un-Islamic.

Ta'zieh quickly outgrew any folkloristic elements. It is an art of civilization, of the towns—a religious art, but neither Canonical nor Classical. In the nineteenth century the Qajar courtiers took up and patronized *ta'zieh* not only to demonstrate their piety but also because the orthodox ulema had always opposed the idea of theater. The Passion Play thus became a pawn in the struggle between ulema and throne for power and prestige in a Shiite monarchy. After the Constitutional Revolution in 1906, *ta'zieh* lost its imperial patronage and went more or less underground. Reza Shah outlawed it, along with the extreme self-flagellation that often accompanied it. In this, for once, throne and ulema agreed. It seemed that *ta'zieh* was doomed.

A few troupes survived however, and under the late Mohammad Reza Shah one heard of performances both amateur and professional given every year, despite the official ban. Finally the Shah lifted even that last obstacle, and the Empress ordered that one Festival of the Arts in Shiraz be devoted to performances by several major professional troupes. Perhaps once again the throne sought to demonstrate piety in opposition to the ulema—who naturally grumbled about the Festival. In any case, the Empress was seen to weep openly at several performances. (*Ta'zieh* is of course "applauded" only with gales of tears and choruses of moans.)

Ta'zieh undoubtedly owes much to pre-Islamic rites of mourning for Tammuz or Adonis or various other dying-resurrecting gods of the Mideast. The very idea of theater is so abhorrent to traditional Islam that *ta'zieh* is virtually the only example of Islamic theater.

The Passion Play makes certain conciliatory gestures toward Islamic aniconism, with results that sometimes give it an uncanny resemblance to post-Artaud avant-garde drama. (Peter Brook witnessed and was influenced by *ta'zieh*.) Not only is naturalism avoided, it is totally replaced by symbolism; so that a voyage across the ocean is represented by a man running around a bucket of water. *Ta'zieh* is precisely "ritual theater": extra-canonical and perhaps even heretical ritual.

It was at one time a genuinely popular art, even during its period of Qajar splendor. By the time the Pahlavis adopted it, however, the last vestiges of nineteenth century Shiite populism in Iran were being replaced by a stricter and more universal adherence to the orthodox ulema. The Revolution of 1978 wants to sweep away all such uncontrollable and ambiguous expressions of faith. *Ta'zieh* was probably dying anyway. It is difficult to conceive its survival in an age of television.

Shiite art in general offers many more examples of "popular" forms. During the nineteenth century, under the Qajars, oil paints were introduced from Europe along with the idea of the large painting not meant to illustrate a book. A totally new style of Persian art quickly evolved. Oil paintings were produced on the one hand for courtiers—portraits and secular scenes—and on the other hand for the "people"—religious subjects.

The religious oil paintings grew to be immense, many of them mural-sized. They were displayed in coffeehouses and are therefore called *qaveh-khaneh* paintings. Like miniatures they use no natural perspective, and strive to present extended time rather than momentary time. In fact some of them use a format very similar to comic strips. But the style is far from delicate. Qajar art strikes the eye as "naive", not at all sophisticated, vivid but crude. At its best it can be powerful, even great. But it is not Classical, and certainly not Canonical. The agonies of Husayn and his family are the most popular subject, and blood is the most common color. Shiite painting deals unrelievedly with pain and gore, but *qaveh-khaneh* techniques were used by more secular and cheerful artists to paint less gloomy subjects.

Certain decorative arts of the Qajar period also demonstrate popular religious forms. For example, painted fired ceramic tile on *ta'zieh* theaters and sufi *khaneqahs;* papier-maché pen-boxes and book-covers; representational carpets; behind-glass paintings; lithographs for books and popular prints. Where sufi influence is felt, the gloom is largely banished; and of course where Qajar influence is felt the atmosphere becomes downright frivolous.

All of this however, whether specifically Shiite or not, is of dubious orthodoxy. Popular Shiism often veers toward extremism and eventually heresy. The ever-recurring and totally heretical notion of Ali's actual divinity, and the Christic aspect of Husayn, lend a decidedly iconic flavor to Shiite popular art which is not at all condoned by the orthodox "Twelver" Shiite ulema. They may tolerate it perforce but they do not condone it.

Khomeini and the revolutionaries specifically evoked images from popular religion, so much so that the more conservative ulema were known to disapprove. The rhetoric of '78 often seemed to suggest a *ta'zieh*-like situation of martyrdom, of Good vs. Evil. Photographs of gun-carrying heros, fountains of blood, vicious SAVAK agents, etc., consciously or unconsiously evoked the heroics and agonies of coffee-house art. Parades of black-veiled women recreated the pictures of Husayn's Household, marching on the court of the wicked Caliph to protest against impious oppression. Millenarian expectations were aroused. Despite Khomeini's puritanism, he makes use of popular religion and even mysticism to create a politics of Images and Archetypes. The outward and artistic expressions of popular religion and sufism are now banned, but their influence continues to flow through other channels.

4. The Tongue of the Unseen

Does there exist a popular religious music in Islam, parallel with popular religious art? The attitude of the strictly orthodox limits the enjoyment of music to those rare occasions, such as weddings, when the Prophet himself is said to have listened with pleasure. Otherwise it is forbidden.

The attitude of the sufis toward *sama'* or Audition (of spiritual music) has already been made clear in earlier chapters. In a phrase, they ask who is listening to the music? and for what purpose? Music is "banned" in Islam because, say the sufis, it is too powerful for secular use. But if it is used as an adjunct to the Path, then it becomes permissable.

The stricter sufi Orders limit themselves to chanting and perhaps drumming. In Persia, India, Turkey and elsewhere, much more elaborate musical services are given, involving whole small orchestras, vocalists and dance—and even written scores. The Mevlevi *sama'* may be the best known of this kind, but the Indian *qawwal* often attains just as high a level of artistry.

In fact, in Islamic civilization sufism and music constantly feed each other. Persian classical music simply could not exist without sufism; indeed, it developed as an initiatic technique for chanting and accompanying mystical texts. I have never heard Persian classical music set to anything but love poetry or chivalric romance. The less strict Orders such as the Kakhsariyya, Ahl-i Haqq, or Safi-Ali-Shahi Nematollahiyya, often seem like mystical music-appreciation societies. They foster virtuosos, and the wealthier brethren hire professional musicians to entertain at *majalis*.

The late Ustad Ilahi, a Kurdish Pir of the Ahl-i Haqq who lived in Tehran, played the three-stringed tambour and invented an entire new system of classical modes. By the end of his life he had almost given up playing, but I once heard a bootleg tape of a private performance for high initiates: a combination of Kurdish strength and Persian delicacy, modal in structure but recognizably not in any standard *dastgah*. . .and brilliantly complex. Ilahi at one time or another attracted many of the best younger traditional musicians to his *jam'-khaneh,* including Dariush Safvat, founder of an Institute to preserve and foster classical music, funded by the Empress and connected to the National Television (which led to bizarre and unusual T.V. programs, to be sure). Other sufi masters used to hire or invite Ahl-i Haqq musicians to entertain them.

The Safi-Ali-Shahi musicians belonged to an older and more professional generation. Many played on Radio Tehran in the old days, and some of them were real masters. They were rumored to smoke opium at their meetings. The Kakhsariyya or "Dust-Heads", who hover on the brink of heresy, feel a special reverence for the Shirazi poet Hafez, whose poems are meant to be chanted. Indeed, it would be impossible to imagine sufism in Shiraz without music—although under Khomeini neither sufism nor music are thriving. The annual celebrations given by Javad Nurbakhsh of the Nematollahiyya in Tehran, where professional musicians "jammed" while Kurdish dervishes whirled in trance—and 2000 people were fed a free hot meal—these fests no longer take place. Women musicians are forbidden to perform at all. Most of the younger professionals have fled the country. Twenty more years of the Islamic Republican Party could kill Persian music forever.

However, sufi music is not necessarily "popular religious" music. In Persia and Turkey it is quite Classical, even Canonical to a certain degree, and played for an elite. It is never performed in mosques, and thus technically speaking it might be considered Classical as opposed to Canonical—but music played in sufi *khaneqahs* is not the sort of music one ordinarily hears on the radio. Nor is it "heterodox"—except to bigots, killjoys and Wahhabis. Sufi music is the aural equivalent of the "abstract" art and calligraphy of Islamic architecture. It belongs to the mainstream and the High Tradition.

Perhaps popular religious music can be found among the Asheks of Anatolia, who sing sufi songs and also revolutionary songs. They are decidedly heterodox, most of them extremist Shiites of some sort. The Ashek world is so rural and agricultural that some might call their art "folkloristic" rather than "popular". But nowadays the Asheks struggle against injustice and are very decidedly of "The People". Their wonderful inventiveness influences Turkish popular music of the radio-and-nightclub variety. The best Asheks are widely known, and sometimes openly persecuted by the State. If Turkey were run by mullas, the Asheks would fare even worse.

When does a religious artform cease to be Classical and become popular? If ten thousand people flock to a sufi shrine in Lahore to hear *qawwali* music which combines folk and classical techniques, improvisation, great emotional appeal and stunning virtuosity, performed in a festival atmosphere, sometimes involving ensembles of a dozen or so singers and musicians—then surely such music might be called both religious and popular. True, Bombay "filmi" music is much more popular. But by making concessions to dubious taste (such as the horrible squeeze-box harmonium) Indian *qawwals* have kept their art alive, if not precisely thriving. A great artist such as the gargantuan Fath Ali Khan of Pakistan blends the most exquisite Classical technique with an explosion of soul—like a combination of Mozart with some hot gospel group from Alabama. He weighs about four hundred pounds, and his hands move like butterflies. When I saw him in Lahore (at the *'urs* or celebration at the shrine of

Data Ganj Bakhsh), rupee notes rained down on him by the thousand, and members of the audience collapsed in ecstatic trances.

Indian music offers many examples of syncretism, for the Classical music of the North is in fact a hybrid of Persian and native traditions. Pious Moslems (such as the Shiite Dagar brothers of Calcutta) sing Hindu temple music; pious Hindus sing the *ghazals* of Hafez. The Bauls of Bengal, a syncretistic sect influenced by tantra, sufism, Advaita and Krishna-worship, create songs of such great beauty that Rabindinath Tagore quietly helped himself to their bounty. Kathak dancing, popularized by the Moghuls, combines Persian influences and Hindu-inspired imagery: a refined form of the *nautch*. Hindu masters teach Moslem students, and vice versa. In Hinduism, musicians are considered low-caste, while Islam is suspicious of their orthodoxy. In India many musicians have escaped into a loose mystical syncretism, replete with bhang, opium and wine—an aristocracy of talent, tolerant and cultivated, breathing the atmosphere of a Moghul past that has never quite vanished from India. The whole country is pervaded by religion: even toothpaste and cigarettes are called "Shiva" and "Ganesh" or "Kaaba" and "Zem-Zem". Bombay churns out films based on the Ramayana and Mahabharata. Popular religious art and music thrive there because religion itself is popular.

The great Egyptian chanteuse Oum Kalsoum usually used sufi lyrics for her songs, even poems by Ibn al-Farid. She sang with not only a full traditional orchestra but a full Western orchestra as well—but her powerful voice easily dominated this mish-mash, and her innate musicality turned popular music—almost cabaret music— into real art. Arabs and Moslems all over the world literally swooned by the thousands at her concerts. I have heard it rumored that she and her composer, Abdul Wahhab, were serious practising sufis; also that she smoked prodigious quantities of hashish. Oum Kalsoum spawned numerous imitators (nearly all of them as corpulant as she) but none of her quality. Several women sufis in Iran have also attained popularity as cabaret performers.

The greatest of all Persian poets, Jaloloddin Rumi, found inspiration even in the simplest folk melodies and banal love-lyrics of his time. Now, through artists like Oum Kalsoum, through radio and recordings, sufism in turn re-nourishes popular music. Back and forth, back and forth, till no one is sure whether the song is about the girl (or boy) next door—or the divine Beloved. One can hear angels sing even on the radio, as if it were indeed (as the Arabs call it) the Tongue of the Unseen.

5. Anonymous Visions
(Commentaries on some of the Plates)

Al-Buraq an-Nabi (Plate 3)

A goddess always hovers just outside the center of any patriarchal monotheism: the Shekinah in Judaism, Sophia in Orthodoxy, the Virgin in Catholicism. For a short time in early Meccan Islam some confusion existed over the roles of Umm and Lazat, two pagan goddesses who almost survived as consorts of al-Lah, the (one) God. In a sense Islam represents a culmination of male spirituality. But its very virility assures the hidden goddess great power. The veiled wife metaphorizes the *baten,* the feminine esoteric, the occult anima. She rules the home, which is ideally centered around an enclosed courtyard with a fountain, like paradise. Ayesha, the Prophet's wife, acts as a sort of Patroness of Sunnism; while Fatima, his daughter, attains a status in Shiism not unlike that of Mary in Christianity. Some sufis, such as Ruzbehan Baqli of Shiraz, and Rumi, revered the mother of Jesus as a symbol of the mystic's heart. Ibn Arabi was initiated into sufism by a woman, and called sexuality the perfect form of contemplation.

Even at its most austere and virile, Islamic art begins to find its feminine nature. Devoid of imagery, the art and architecture of Granada, Damascus, Isfahan and Delhi attained a femininity—an eroticism—which caused the first European visitors to find these cities depraved and luxurious. Christian art—which depicts the figure—can never contain such open celebration of the erotic as the garden of the Alhambra, or the roofscape of Yazd (in southern Iran) which seems made of flesh, desert-colored flanks, thighs and breasts punctuated by phallic wind-towers and minarets.

One would expect an anima to emerge very clearly in popular—as opposed to Canonical/Classical—Islamic art. Cheap lithographs give expression to the unofficial aspects of a faith. The figure of Buraq already exists in ancient miniatures, but almost always in a secondary role, as the Prophet's magical mount. In this print from Bombay, however, the creature appears by herself as an icon which can be contemplated in its own right.

The Prophet was transported from Mecca instanta-neously one night to the Dome of the Rock in Jerusalem, and from there rode to heaven on Buraq. The *mir'aj* or Night Ascension is a favorite theme with sufi poets and artists. A version translated into Latin is supposed to have helped inspire Dante's *Divina Commedia*. A famous *Shahnameh* miniature of the early Safavid School of Tabriz shows the veiled Prophet, his head halo'd by Chinese-style flames, riding through the clouds attended by angels.

Buraq is part mule, part woman, part bird or angel. The mule is an in-between beast, neither donkey nor horse. Buraq herself is neither this nor that, but rather something in-between. She flies between earth and heaven as an angel does, crossing the Isthmus *(barzakh)* between this world and the Other World of Imaginal vision. She carries the Prophet as a shaman's Ally or familiar might carry him up the tentpole and into the sky. She represents animal nature, human mind and angelic inspiration, spanning the rungs on the ladder of creation with ambiguous ease. She is the Muse who summons the *vates,* the poet-prophet. She is the Message from beyond our limited perception, the Call to Knowledge. As man rides beautiful woman to the in-stasy of union with the One in love, so does the visionary ride the woman-soul within him: Buraq/Pegasus/Iris/Hermes, psychopompessa, initiatrix, witch-and-broomstick-in-one, triple-natured Hecate, nocturnal ecstasy, envoy of the houris, goddess of night, the esoteric and unseen, who opens the crack between Dimensions.

In this Bombay version the background appears Kashmiri (trees, lake, Moghul domes and palaces). Bombay has a traditional link with Kashmir, now reinforced by countless "talkies" with love-scenes set in lush cool valleys of the north. An attempt at perspective reveals Western influence but fails to erase the essential flatness of the composition—which is emphasized by the calligraphy and also by the cut-out pasted-up look of Buraq herself. The Prophet's living vehicle appears very like the classical model the artist has copied, although her face is distinctly that of a Moghul princess (or courtesan). Her trappings include a Persian saddle-cloth, a Kashmiri shawl and some eighteenth-century Moghul jewelry.

By omitting the Dome of the Rock, the angels and the Prophet himself from the image, the artist comes perilously close to creating an idol—an Islamic and feminine Garuda. She is freed from her story, her particular myth, and takes on a life of her own. She seems to invite the mystic to envision himself in her saddle, to participate in the Prophetic Light. She is the vehicle of dream—and Mohammad said, "A veridical dream is the fortieth part of prophecy."

Jagged, violent, hallucinatory, *The Black Div* ("Devil") is the work of a brilliant naive artist. Brilliant, but not very well balanced, the rug recalls paintings produced by talented inmates of lunatic asylums. But, mad as it is, the piece is certainly no random production of a distorted mind. It is rich in traditional symbolism—of a rather sinister variety—and may be the work of one of Iran's "Devil-Worshippers" *(Shaytan-parastiyyan)*.

The scene is divided into three levels: In the air an eagle with multi-colored feathers carries off a lamb; on earth a blue lion with a rainbow mane gnaws the haunch of a red stag amidst a landscape of dead logs overgrown with fungus; a blue fox looks on hungrily, a pair of rabbits, blue and red, timidly.

"Between" earth and heaven, however, a split has opened in the fabric of reality. The eagle has drawn the attention of two djinn, who have half-materialized themselves out of the World of Archetypes. One of them threatens the eagle with an arrow—or perhaps a thunderbolt. A lion is about to fall out of the sky; his claws can be seen entering the picture from above. The air rains flowers.

On the mountaintop, at the focus of the composition, the Black Div strides or prances. He leads a wild blue stallion, and a minor blue djinn or monkey hangs to his tail. A hand, or an ebony cock's-comb, protrudes from his forehead. A red goat lifts its hooves in a gesture of worship toward the satanic figure.

Around the border demon masks leer and beasts devour one another: a motif common in Persian art since pre-Islamic times, but here carried to an unpleasantly obsessive extreme.

The theory that this carpet may be the work of devil-worshippers (rather than a mere illustration to some folk tale or the *Shahnameh*) originated with the late Henry Corbin, the great French philosopher and scholar of Persian religion. The pre-Islamic Avestan faith of Iran, he recalled, tended towards a kind of dualism. It posited a cosmic struggle between the forces of Good, represented by Ahura Mazda, the Holy Spirit, and Evil, represented by his twin brother Ahriman. According to Zoroaster, Good must finally prevail, and the duty of man is to aid it and follow its precepts.

But Ahriman is the Prince of this world, and there are always those who will deal with him for gain, or for the sheer perverse intellectual pleasure of opposing all that is light and reasonable.

Some historians believe that European witchcraft was not inherently evil, but represented the survival of pagan worship amongst the peasants of remote corners of the West, for whom Christianity was the religion of foreign conquerors. In Iran too it would be easy for remnants of pre-Zoroastrian cults to linger on in mountain valleys, and natural for the cultists to identify their own god with Ahriman, the official Enemy of the official deity, Ahura Mazda.

Many of these pocket-cults must have survived into the Islamic era, resisting the new religion of Light just as they had always resisted the old. By this time, however, they would have forgotten their "pagan" origins and come to think of themselves as devil-worshippers—just as their old enemies had labelled them.

Islam too has its devil: Iblis or Shaitan, the great fallen angel who, according to the Koran, refused to bow down at God's command and worship the newly-created Adam. But Islam has nothing in it of dualism. God is One, he has created everything, even Iblis. Like all monotheisms, therefore, Islam is faced with the difficulty of explaining why a good God would allow evil to exist.

For the mystics the answer is simple—but shocking. If God is One, then all things are manifestations of his divinity—even the devil. Mansur al-Hallaj explained that Iblis refused to bow before Adam because he was a true lover of God's unity, and could not worship a mere creation. Satan, therefore, is the perfect monotheist. In heaven he preached God's unity to the angels. On earth, after his "fall", he preaches blackness to man, only because man cannot know Light without Dark. At the end of profane Time, Iblis will be saved, brought back to perfect oneness with God. He is, in fact, the very image of the Hallajian mystic: the lover in agony over his separation from the Beloved.

Hallaj was crucified by the exoteric authorities of Baghdad, and even the sufis called for his death. A later spiritual descendent, Ayn al-Qozat Hamadani (d. 1131), who also wrote of Iblis as the Perfect Lover, was also executed for heresy. But these men had their followers, and not all of them were wiped out. Wandering dervishes carried these strange doctrines with them. Shaykh Adi of Baalbek, for example, journeyed from Baghdad up into the farthest mountains of Iraq, where he discovered a pagan sect called the Yezidis. They worshipped a peacock angel, Malek Ta'us, whom they identified as the devil. Shaykh Adi remained with them and initiated them into his own brand of shaitanic esotericism.

In Iran, in Kurdestan, similar sects had survived the centuries of Islam. Another wandering dervish named Sultan Ishaq founded a new religion based partly on sufism and partly on paganism, called the Ahl-i Haqq, "People of Truth". One branch of this new faith must have come into contact with a sufi preaching the doctrines of Hallaj and Hamadani, for they became devil-worshippers, Shaitan-parastiyyan. According to their Moslem neighbors they eat pork and drink wine and live by brigandage; they are also accused, like so many other heretics, of "extinguishing the lamps" and indulging in orgies of polymorphous perversion. In fact, modern travellers find them simple mountain people, ignorant but kind. Their greeting, instead of "Peace be with you", is "Hail, Essence of Satan!"

Iblis will be "saved at the end of Time"; even the orthodox believe this. Prophetic hadith deal extensively with the final abolition of Hell, as if to counterbalance all the brimstone of the Koran. Mohammad promised that watercress would grow in the streambeds of Gehenna, and that God would laugh for pleasure as he freed the last soul from perdition ("for God loveth a good jest").

Eschatology—or the belief in life-after-death—solves the problem of evil for orthodox religion. Only beyond Time can true unity be attained. Evil is allowed its shadow-existence so that humans will look to their immortal souls and prepare themselves for death and judgement.

The mystic believes that (in the Prophet's words) he can "die before death" and (as a Christian would say) "attain the Beatific Vision in this life." The sufis have called this "converting one's own Iblis to Islam."

If a person attains such a state, one might expect him to adopt an antinomian stance and declare that since "evil" no longer exists for him, then "Do as thou wilt shall be the whole of the Law."

Orthodoxy must reply to this assertion by demanding that all of Revelation be accepted on faith, not merely the esoteric meaning which can be known through presential experience, but also the literal sense of scripture, including the eschatology for which no evidence exists save the testimony of prophetic vision.

Although the Prophet himself advised us to take nothing on mere faith, it would seem that orthodox authority might disintegrate unless this literal sense is accepted with unquestioning belief. Moslems boast that they do not "believe because it is absurd"—but finally the existence of the immortal soul (in the sense of an identity to be punished or rewarded or reincarnated or whatever) rests on no argument stronger than this credo. The axiom of Unity *(tawhid)* cannot be used to prove the reality of heaven and hell. In fact, the metaphysics of Advaita—

unhampered by dogma—carries the principle of Oneness to a different conclusion, and denies all reality even to the notion of individual existence.

The Islamic heretic accepts Revelation as a kind of code which must be broken, in both the cryptographical and the legal senses of the word "break". The absurd notion of eternal punishment cannot be literally true (even if the torture will end when Time itself halts); hell can only be a metaphor for the misery we suffer now, much of it the result of our illusions, our lack of attention to the real. Similarly the notion of paradise can only have meaning as a symbol of what consciousness may attain here and now.

The world is veiled in illusion caused by our forgetfulness of the real, and also by the limitation of our senses. Nevertheless the world itself—even the world we so imperfectly perceive—is not only real but also the very means of "attaining salvation"—or rather, realization. The world *(dunya)* which must be transcended and the self *(nafs)* which must be purified are already—in and of themselves—perfect manifestations of the Oneness of Being.

So Shaitan is already "saved". Iblis represents the very principle of multiplicity which, for the mystic, has become the key to unity. Iblis "rules this world" of shadow and light and directs the play which liberates us, which allows us to pull ourselves by our own bootstraps up out of the slavery of illusion. To those still wrapped in delusion he appears as a devil, the evil in which we lose ourselves and destroy our true joy. To the esotericist however he manifests as Lucifer, Light-bearer, image of initiatory and liberating truth.

The color black resonates with positive and esoteric symbolism in Persian culture. As in the West, the negative aspects are known: mourning and death, "black" magic and devils, negro slavery and so on. But black is also the color of the banners of the Household of the

Prophet. Black is the color of *fana'*, Annihilation in the Real. "The Sun at Midnight", a phrase familiar in Western alchemy, is also used in sufi poetry. *Nur-i siyah*, "Black Light", represents either the highest stage of the mystic's path, or the penultimate stage. (See Corbin's *Man of Light in Iranian Sufism* for the argument over this point. If black is the second-highest stage, then green is used to symbolize the most exalted.) The Hidden Imam of orthodox Shiism always appears in visions as a young man dressed in black.

Moreover, not all divs or djinn are evil. Some of them were converted by Solomon and others by the Prophet (these latter are said to have fought for Imam Husayn at Karbala, and are often depicted in the *Ta'zieh*). Despite their fearsome aspect and fiery nature these good djinn willingly assist the "white magician" in his spiritual and ceremonial magic. (Looked at from this point of view, the tale of Aladdin and the Lamp can be seen as a sufi instruction story.) As in Tibetan tantra, so in Islamic esotericism, devils only terrify those who are afraid of facing their own forgetfulness. For the initiate even the most horrendous demons become benevolent tutelary spirits, symbols of the Thunderbolt Power.

The "Black Div" carpet might or might not owe inspiration to some of the lore and teaching of the heretics sketched in above. Perhaps after all it is no more than a rather bizarre artistic fancy. But the enigmatic forces of its design suggest something more than mere fancy— something born of dark mountain valleys and the half-forgotten rites of gnostic ancestors. Whatever the artist's conscious intentions, this rug could serve as an illustration to Hallaj's *Kitab al-tawasin* or to some folktale about the Yezidis or Devil-worshippers of Kurdestan. Its terroristic imagery could be "evil" in intent, or "benevolent" as the bloodthirsty Kali herself, with her necklace of skulls. The rug's power is only augmented and enhanced by its spooky ambiguity.

Semar as Allah (Plate 4—5)

Aside from the major civilizations of India and China, Indonesia (particularly Java) is the richest East Asian source for popular religious art. Shamanism, Buddhism and Hinduism are all still present, overlaid and refined by Islam. The result is a syncretistic religious art of great subtlety and force.

A major focus for Javanese culture is the Wayang Kulit, the shadow puppet play based on the Hindu epics, the Ramayana and Mahabharata, but enlivened with local additions. Under Islamic influence the puppet forms were abstracted and elaborated, and as archetypes are seen everywhere in Java, on shop signs and posters and magazines. Wayang Kulit is truly popular: even today the repertory is being expanded by brilliant improvisatory puppeteers (called *dalangs*), and everyone from the rickshaw driver to the sultan still enjoys their work and knows their names. The Wayang serves as a vehicle for Javanese self-consciousness: the plays both reflect and shape political, social and spiritual forces in Java. They are religious and chivalric in origin and theme, and also serve as teaching-aids on the spiritual paths of many Kebatinan mystics. Ordinary playgoers are often quite aware of the basic symbolism of the plays, but the mystics enjoy performing hermeneutics and meditating on yogic secrets revealed by the material. But since Java is "officially" Islamic and because of the influence of Moslem reformist puritanism, Wayang Kulit is not and cannot be considered a Canonical religious art, even though it was used and enjoyed by sufis in the past; but it is in effect a perfect example of popular religious art.

When the Nine Walis of Indonesia decided to make use of traditional Hindu-Buddhist-Shamanic artforms to propagate Islam and sufism, they chose in particular the Wayang Kulit—so goes the story—and as a natural result the form of the puppets as well as certain aspects of the performance itself underwent a transformation. The aniconic tendency of Islam manifested itself in an exaggerated abstraction of form and a proliferation of decorative motifs, so that the puppets became more and more "spiritual"—attenuated, non-representational, graceful and eccentric to the point of a hallucinatory vividness of design. As for the Walis, they became characters in the storehouse of myth that shapes the various Wayang performances.

This story is denied by some scholars who say that the initial aesthetic impulse in this special direction came to Java earlier than Islam, under the thirteenth century Hindu King Raden Panji Inukertapati of Jenggala, and that the continued development of Wayang forms has been influenced much less by Islam than the early European scholars believed.

If this "pre-Islamic" theory is true, one might expect a closer resemblance between Javanese and Balinese versions of the Wayang; whereas, in fact, all the differences between the two seem reducible to the influence of Islam in Java and its absence from Bali. Aside from this however, it seems to me that the either/or approach to a truly popular art form such as Wayang Kulit—the insistence that it must be either Islamicized or nationalized—simply misses the point. In the creatively syncretistic culture of Java, both Islamic and Hindu-Javanese aesthetics are obviously woven together in the shadow-forms; but the result is a coherent and integrated artform within a coherent and integrated cultural matrix. A similar spirit can be felt in the music of North India, for example, where a precise and elegant sense of ornamentation and abstraction—typical of Persian mysticism and art—weds a musical system and a certain cosmological scope native to India. Sufism must find congenial the whole metaphysic of shadows which gave rise to the Wayang in the first place. But finally, the compatibility of Islam and the Wayang is "proved" by the existence of calligrams (such as

"Semar as Allah") in which figures from the drama are depicted in the forms of Arabic lettering, often with clear mystical resonances.

Islamic art strives to fill—completely and densely— the entire imaginative space offered by two dimensions. What "disturbs" Islam is the illusion of a third dimension, for only "real things" can fill "real space". In its extreme form this aesthetic denies the illusion of the fourth dimension as well; and without the expansion of temporality drama becomes impossible, and music presents certain difficulties as well. Sufism, which in a broad sense is responsible for the very introduction of Islam to many non-Arabs, interprets this aesthetic in the positive sense of an intensification of vision rather than in the negative sense of a prohibition of images. It seeks for this special vision in the cultures it meets, and learns to express itself in modes and artforms which in strict orthodox terms are questionable or even forbidden. In Wayang Kulit, Time— and therefore drama—becomes possible because of the very flatness of the shadows, because the illusion or distortion of Time in a two-dimensional world results not in the representtion of "ordinary" or "secular" temporality but rather in the evocation of another sort of Time altogether: dream-time, myth-time, archetype-time, mystical time, atemporal time.

The Wayang puppets represent a triumph of two-dimensional art rivalled only by Egyptian painting and Islamic "decoration" (in quotation marks because what Western art considers mere decoration and therefore secondary is in fact absolutely central in the Islamic aesthetic). Made of painted skin, the puppets are totally and undeniably flat. Skindeep. The very nature of the artform—shadow-play—involves the implementation of an image with no thickness whatsoever. Whoever developed the Javanese Wayang in its present form, and whatever the influence of sufism, the purpose of this development was to "solve" two-dimensionality, to free it of any vestige of an illusory third dimension, to purify it in fact, and allow it to express fully what it intends to express. Chinese, Thai, Malay and even Balinese Wayang forms do not carry the logic of structure to such a realized conclusion. They still deal to a certain extent with silhouettes rather than shadows; thus they are simultaneously more representational and more static and regular than the Javanese forms. In other words: a silhouette implies a solid body; a shadow, cut off from its "archetype", suggests only what can be contained by utter flatness.

The elongated arms and faces of the Javanese forms express an imaginal potentiality of movement which contains too much energy to impress the eye with a sense of rigidity. The puppets are not meant to represent the mere remnants or cast-off reflections of "real" three-dimensional models. The Wayang puppets occupy a reference-space or world of their own, a Flatland realm of pure shadow (rather like the shadows of people in certain fairy tales which take on lives of their own).

The revolution in Javanese Wayang aesthetic, whenever and however it occured, made the puppets more than merely the shades of the ancestors. In formal terms they are cut off from all systems except the topology of flatness. In metaphysical terms they are the archetypes. Because of their very flatness the figures escape all restrictions of space as we experience it. Like ghosts or spirits they can alter their shapes—and when they shift shape in ways that open up a new world of perception, a different world, they become analogues of spiritual vision. Given the premise of the shadow-play, the Javanese forms seem somehow necessary and inevitable, not just as expressions of a given culture but as the inescapable products of a search for beauty without illusory depth.

From this point of view it is not the puppets themselves which constitute the artforms but their shadows on the screen. At first it might seem that the symbolism of Wayang Kulit would equate the puppeteer with God in his

creative aspect—Divine Will; the lamp with his "mind"—
Divine Intellect; the puppets with the archetypes; and the
shadows with the world of material creation. (In fact, God
is sometimes called "the Supreme Dalang".)

But if the shadows and not the puppets are the
"point" of the art, then this equation must be reconsid-
ered—not discarded but rather added to. In one sense the
shadows are much more like "ideas" or archetypes than
the puppets, which are after all still objects. Or one might
say that the shadows are the "essences" of the puppets
and hence present their esoteric meaning. The shadows
themselves are the mystery, and what goes on behind the
screen is simply a mechanism for producing the outward
show of secrets, in which the perfection of the phenomena
is completed. This interpretation is borne out by the
Javanese tradition which equates the lamp with "Eternal
Life", the puppets with bodies and the shadows with
souls.

In such a reading the role of the dalang becomes less
theological, more ambiguous and mysterious. He is an in-
between-man, a shaman or priest responsible for mediating between gods and men through his visionary access to
the world of the Imagination. In fact, the Balinese "initiated" dalang is still called a priest, and recites mantras
and calls down the gods as a medium to possess him with
their personalities and virtues. Thus the dalang is an
inner stage of which the outer performance is a shadow.
In this case, God is the fire in the lamp, and the lamp is his
"vehicle", Garuda, the symbol of intuitive knowledge which
"takes flight". (All of which makes the modern substitu-
tion of a naked lightbulb for the traditional Garuda-lamp
somewhat bathetic, symbolically as well as aesthetically
impoverished.)

The dalang's side of the screen is perhaps the most
interesting, since some of the puppet work can only be
appreciated from that side—but with the lantern shining
on the world of colors, the dalang himself is in shadow and

becomes a shade, a silhouette, like the black-garbed puppeteers of Bunraku (by convention invisible). This appears to me as the final twist or reversal of symbols, since now the puppets possess the solidity of color while the dalang has vanished into insubstantiality, not a god or sorcerer but simply a disembodied voice. At his either hand are ranged and ranked the hundreds of puppets waiting to be breathed to life; at his back sit the orchestra and singers, present only as a dim density of sound (except for the clouds of clove-scented tobacco smoke they puff into the pool of light, like incense at a ritual.) At the center of the composition sits the dalang, a black shadow, all negative capability, all pure potential, dark hole in the middle of this tiny nocturnal cosmos which exists only between the night and dawn prayers: that portion of the earth's cycle given over to meditation, or to dreams.

In the Wayang Kulit the Imaginal World itself—the scene where the action transpires—is represented by the one "inanimate" prop in the dalang's collection: the kekayon or gunungan (mountain), which on Bali is called Babad or "the story". It is the abode of gods, goddesses and demons, and thus the vortex out of which the narrative flows and by which it is rendered sacred. As a scene-divider the gunungan is pointed to the left before midnight, straight up at midnight and to the right thereafter, symbolizing the progress of the spiritual path. During the performance it serves as mountain, river, forest, fire, wind, water, ocean, heaven or hell, beginning and end. But aside from this multiplicity it also represents the highest unity, or rather the point at which multiplicity and Imagination intersect with the absolute Unity of Being:

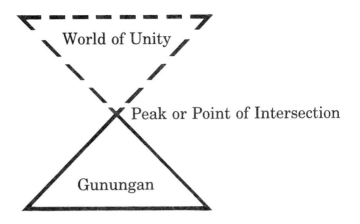

World of Unity

Peak or Point of Intersection

Gunungan

Thus it is Mount Meru, on top of which Shiva sits in rapt meditation, the water of life flowing from his forehead. Within the gunungan is the design of a tree of life, an Indian fig, sacred to Shiva—which to a Moslem would at once suggest the "Lote Tree of Farthest Limit" which divides the lower heavens of the Imagination from the higher paradise of pure unity, its branches alive with the images of life. In fact the gunungan closely resembles the Persian tree of life, which is lozenge or cypress-shaped, guarded at the trunk by two lions (the gunungan has two giants with war-clubs), its branches festooned with dragons, birds and other figures—just as in Java.

The element of Time in Wayang is structured on two lines—narration and music—which are woven into a single braid. That is, the narration is shared by the dalang to a certain extent with the female vocalist and with the gamelan. In the portion of the drama when the dalang creates dialogue he is usually accompanied by a single line of improvisation on one of the metalophones, and provides his own staccato rhythm with a metal clapper and a wooden stick; so that the entire performance, from sunset to dawn, possesses the wholeness of a single piece of music stretched out with a great many spoken words.

Excessive length and a certain amount of formal monotony characterize nearly all traditional drama, whether aristocratic or popular. Kathakali also goes on all night, cycles of Noh plays can go on for days at a time, Chinese opera and Kabuki, all are very long. At the various forms of Wayang drama the audiences come and go, eat, drink, play with babies, chat and sleep, wake up for the exciting bits, nod off again. The art for some is woven into the life of the evening, like a celebration, and into the life of the night, like a dream—while others, the cognoscenti, appreciate subtle effects and sophisticated techniques.

Length and monotony, virtues in a more traditional ambience, lose their appeal in competition with movies and television, because these media are easier, less time-consuming, and make very little demand on the active imagination of the audience. Wayang Kulit is of course disappearing, like other old-fashioned long-drawn-out Oriental forms of drama. Attempts are being made to preserve it (pickle it) for posterity. But on the whole it still has some life in it and is not quite ready for the museum yet (although there already exists a wonderful Wayang Museum in Djakarta). At least one radio station in Jogjakarta broadcasts Wayang all night—within earshot of my hotel.

Javanese Wayang Kulit fits the definition of popular religious art so seamlessly that it could serve as a prototype or touchstone against which to test other artforms. As a survival of Hinduism in an Islamic culture it must by definition be extra-canonical. Yet it embodies the quintessence of Javanese mystical sentiment and does so quite openly, since it was mystical to begin with (the *Bagavad Gita* is the heart of the *Mahabharata,* which in turn is the heart of the Wayang cycle); moreover, this mysticism seems to have been refined and elaborated later under the influence of sufism and kebatinan, the "Javanese Path". Some of the mystics were also kings, and Wayang had its royal patrons and even performers (like Kathakali). But its appeal is without doubt popular and is recognized as such by the Indonesians themselves. The government, for example, uses certain dalangs as mouthpieces for its propaganda. Wayang may have started as a tribal art (ritual ancestor worship perhaps) and has certainly been shaped in part by a "High" traditional aesthetic, but the result is a form with appeal for every level of Javanese society.

The popularization of Wayang, or perhaps even its "democratization", is symbolized by the character who in a sense plays the central role: Semar, chief and father of the Panakawan or clown-servants who accompany the heroic Pandawa brothers. Semar is grotesque in the extreme, as are his progeny. Freaks used to be considered propitious in Java and were given positions as court jesters. The Panakawan are bumpkins, wiseacres, alternately foolish and only seemingly foolish—rather like Mulla Nasreddin and other civilized Trickster-figures. They are not found in the *Mahabharata* but are a purely Javanese addition to the cycle, their origin unknown, their repertoire of jokes changing with the time and its follies. All the satirical humor, social commentary and even political fervor of the Javanese people are contained in the clowns—who were avid supporters of Indonesian Independence, for example, during the war with the Dutch. Semar has become something of a symbol of Java—the "dark shadow" on the other side of the coin of Garuda, the official symbol of state (both of Indonesia and the island of Java). Semar speaks for Everyman. But he is also a manifestation of *Betara Ismaya,* Divine Omniscience. Quite often he gets the Pandawas out of the tangles they have made of their chivalry and honor and romantic love. He is the highest, disguised as the lowest.

From the purely formal point of view, Semar's is the most perfectly two-dimensional of all the shadows, a compositional topograph around which the bony angles of the other figures seem to converge. He is the world itself, *Maya,* in both its positive sense and its sense of absurdity; both guardian of those who meditate, and an object of contemplation in himself. He stands for a feeling in Javanese mysticism that high and low must meet, must not conflict with each other, that the ordinary and even the ugly have a non-ordinary luminescence about them which is needed to balance the elegance of royalty and the ascetism of saints.

According to my sorcerer friend, Pak H--- of Solo (see Chapter One), the characters of Wayang represent aspects of Kundalini Yoga. He says Semar stands for the Crown Chakra, not the Genital or Muladhara Chakra as stated in most commentaries. Perhaps one might say that Semar represents the lowest point of the "Serpent of Power", the genitals, in his outward manifestation, and the highest in his divine manifestation. Thus he symbolizes the whole path, the entire "process" of Kundalini, the axis around which the other characters revolve as well as the "ladder" by which they attain to higher consciousness.

The figure of "Semar as Allah" (Pl. 4) sums up the entire relation of sufism and the Wayang. Painting behind glass is a common form of naive and popular art, found for example in Qajar Persia and twentieth century Taiwan. Rastika of Cirembon works in a Javanese tradition but with authentic individual genius. He always paints Wayang figures, and many of his pieces depict them in orgiastic and polymorphous-perverse sexual play: amazing tantrik pornography! "Semar as Allah" is a traditional Islamic-Javanese theme: the body of the hermaphrodite albino hunchback is composed entirely of the Arabic word, "Allah", written over and over again. The repetition of the divine Name, the *zekr* or invocation, makes up the very flesh of the image.

The garments and detailed figuration are treated in the sinuous and baroque style of Wayang puppets, and the background is Islamic green. I do not denigrate Rastika's art by calling it hallucinogenic, for it is utterly and crystallinely controlled. I only wish I could afford to introduce the large erotic canvasses to the West, since I believe Rastika to be a great artist and a validation of the continuing vitality of Javanese tradition.

Semar is Allah is Brahma is Java is a freak and a clown. The Javanese live inside his wild and tricky laughter, his peasant wisdom, his wisecracks, his luminous and divine Unity. All this Rastika has understood and expressed without the slightest hesitation or doubt. Everything I have to say in this book is already prefigured in this painting: a scandal, a secret that was not meant to be unveiled, a flowering of the divine-mad Imagination, the paradoxical, the erotic, the insane.

7

A Note on the Use of Wine, Hemp & Opium

The Shariah forbids all intoxicants. A Moslem who drinks wine or uses hashish acts against the Shariah, but someone who uses an intoxicant for spiritual purposes can rightly be called not just a sinner but a heretic.

Nevertheless a great many people in Iran, Afghanistan, Pakistan, India and elsewhere use preparations of cannabis for various spiritual reasons. Very little has been published on this subject, and of that little almost nothing of value. Between 1968 and 1978 I had occasion to observe and participate in such hemp use, and I consider my own observations of some small value.

In the Subcontinent, one concoction often used spiritually is called bhang. Cannabis is sacred to Shiva in Hinduism, and on his major annual feast-day (so I was told) even the most pious Hindu may consume a glass of bhang. In Shiva's sacred city of Benares, bhang is sold on the streets in the form of a delicious ice-cream *(bhang kulfi melai)* as well as in sherbets and pastilles. Shaivite saddhus smoke cannabis as well, often in the form of ganja mixed with tobacco and consumed in chilams—although they smoke charas when they can get it.

Ganja is the flowering bud of the female plant.

Bhang is the palmate leaf or "shade-leaf" in modern American slang.

Hashish (Arabic for "grass") or charas is a preparation of pollen and resinous dust, ideally transformed into cakes by heat and manipulation—any other admixture or process resulting in an inferior product. The buds of the harvested Indica plants are dropped gently on a fine silk scarf and the very purest pollen thus separated and saved. Subsequent and inferior grades of charas are made by forcing the cannabis through silk and then cotton. The highest grade, sometimes called *shireh* or essence, was always saved (according to legend) for the growers themselves, or for gifts to *maulangs* (holy men or dervishes) or to the king—who always got the best of everything. I can attest that *maulangs* often seem to smoke only the very finest of north Afghan charas, the black/gold/green from the valleys between Herat and Balkh. Now that the Soviet Army has become accustomed to hashish of this quality, interesting changes should begin to occur in Russian society: another parallel with U.S. experience in Viet Nam.

Chilam—a stemless pipe, usually stone or fired clay, conical, the narrow end partly blocked by a loose pebble. The ganja and tobacco are chopped, washed and squeezed dry. A hot coal keeps the pipe lit. A bit of cloth wrapped around the base prevents residue from reaching the smoker's mouth. Smoking a chilam is a complex process and needs to be demonstrated rather than described; each smoker develops his own personal style.

Charas is widely used by Afghan *maulangs* or wandering dervishes, and is also more generally available in north Pakistan (Baluchistan, N.W. Frontier, Kafiristan, Swat, Chitral) than elsewhere in the Subcontinent. It is smoked in large water-pipes with tulip-shaped bowls of fired clay, often bound with metal wire for extra strength. Some of these pipes are so large one must stand up to smoke them, and I have heard of pipes that were built into the floor and had to be smoked while standing on a stool. Bhang and ganja are used by Moslems of the Subcontinent, often even when charas is available, since the effects are slightly different.

Bhang is milder and subtler than the other preparations. In Avicennan parlance, it "cools the blood" and is considered healthier in hot weather than smoking. Also, because it is (usually) consumed as liquid, it reminds the dervishes of wine, the sufi symbol for spiritual intoxication. I came across (and unfortunately lost) a translation of an Indian sufi *Bhang-nama*, a poem in praise of bhang which described it in terms of sufi wine. References to the "green parrot" in sufi literature may sometimes be taken as standing for bhang or hashish.

Since I have never seen an adequate published description of bhang-preparation, I will include the recipe here, with traditional and modern variations. The traditional version comes from a *saki-khaneh* in Quetta, Baluchistan, Pakistan. (*Saki-khaneh,* "House of the Cupbearer". The saki or wine-serving boy is a symbol of the Beloved or the spiritual master in sufi poetry, but in Pakistan *saki-khaneh* is a slang term for a tea-house that serves charas and bhang.) This technique requires three people and much patience.

Take about a half a pound of cannabis, either the shade-leaves from cultivated hashish-plants, or if using very weak quality include the buds as well. Strip away the branches but do not separate the leaves and seeds.

Heat the leaves and seeds on a dry griddle over a low-medium flame till the leaves are crisp and an oily smell begins to arise.

Now wash the greenery in cold water a few times, gently but thoroughly, and squeeze it gently. I was told that the omission of this step causes headaches, but have no empirical proof of that assertion.

Now take a fired clay pot, shaped like this:

capacity at least several gallons. The bottom-inside must be rounded, not flat—and it must have been scored before firing with a crisscross pattern of slightly raised edges or welts.

Place the wet cannabis in the bottom of the pot. At least one person has to hold the pot steady while one other person wields a pestle, a piece of wood about two and a half feet long which can be easily grasped, and with a blunt club-like end. Rotate and grind the bhang with the pestle, using both hands. Get up a good steady stirring rhythm, like paddling in a canoe race. Chant some appropriate folksong. Keep it up for at least two hours.

The following are favorite flavor-additions, to be crushed with the bhang according to taste: almonds, pistachios, cardamons, peppercorns (white and black), cinnamon stick, and any sort of edible seed such as white or black poppy, sunflower, etc.

When the bhang is thoroughly creamed to a superfine paste, scrape it from the pot and put it in a cotton cloth or folded cheesecloth. Hold the edges of the cloth over a pail or bucket (this needs two people) and begin to pour a slow trickle of cold water over the bhang while gently kneading the lump of paste with your fingers. Keep kneading and pouring till the water which dribbles into the bucket is no longer green-tinted. Discard the remaining paste and drink the bucket of liquid—about twenty to forty servings.

In Benares bhang is prepared on a flat rubbing-stone mortar and pestle and sold in small pellets. The poor swallow these pills with water, but the well-to-do dissolve them in milk or lassi with flavored syrups (rose, almond, khas) or sugar and spices.

In the modern technique the hours of grinding and singing may be eliminated by the use of a Cuisinart, Osterizer or other high-speed blender, for about a half an hour. Use Domestic Backlot, or the shade-leaves from sinsemilla, since anything else would be expensive and wasteful—and too powerful.

Perhaps the most impressive spiritual use of bhang I witnessed was at an 'urs or Death-Anniversary celebration at the sufi shrine of Madho Lal Husayn, outside the Shalimar Gardens in Lahore in 1973.

Lal Husayn might well have been included in the chapter on The Witness Game—but since my sources for his life are largely oral, I will describe him here instead. He seems to exemplify the Qalanadar spirit, the way of the wild dervish, intoxicated and erotic.

Husayn was a pious and ascetic sufi who used to spend every night immersed to his waist in the river, reading the Koran. One night however he suddenly laughed and hurled the Book into the water, where it sank beneath the waves.

He shaved his beard and took to wearing bright ruby-red *(lal)* robes, wandering around Lahore spouting poetry and nonsense. One day he saw a beautiful young Brahmin boy named Madho and fell in love with him. After much courting of the boy, and despite resistance from Madho's family, Lal Husayn became his spiritual master and lover.

Some say he converted the whole Hindu family to Islam through a miracle, but a more reliable version claims he had no interest in converting anyone to anything except the supremacy of love, which he extolled in Punjabi lyrics of still-widespread popularity. When they died, Madho and Lal Husayn were buried in the same tomb.

Lahore is said to have seven hundred sufi shrines, and of the many I visited each seemed to possess a different personality. Data Ganj Bakhsh is artistic, pious, royal. Mian Mir is serene, faithful, cool. But Madho Lal Husayn is intoxicated and slightly risqué.

The Qalandariyya are an organized sufi Order in Pakistan, with their center at the tomb of Lal Shabaz Qalandar ("The Ruby Hawk") in Sehwan Sheriff near Hyderabad, Sindh. Certainly all over Afghanistan and Pakistan the most popular prayer before lighting a pipe of charas or taking a cup of bhang is, "Ya! Lal Shabaz Qalandar!"

The 'urs of Mahdo Lal Husayn was decidedly held in this spirit. A great deal of bhang was consumed in a very brotherly—if somewhat insane—ambience. Qawwali music was played and transvestite whirling dervishes performed (see Plate 6). A number of plainly-dressed people said their prayers, but I did not observe any of the *maulangs* join them. Several shaykhs were accompanied by very handsome boys.

The medieval arch-bigot Ibn Taymiyya lumped hashish-eaters in the same damnable category with boy-lovers and sufis. The three tastes appear linked in much Islamic literature. The great Abu Nowas is supposed to have written this Khayyamian quatrain:

> A pound of roast meat, a few loaves of bread
> A jug of wine, at least one willing boy,
> A pipe of hashish. Now the picnic's spread
> My garden beggars paradise's joy.

The following verses are variously attributed to the thirteenth-century Spaniard Ibn Khamis or the twelfth-century Syro-Egyptian Ibn al-A'ma:

> Swear off wine and drink from the cup of
>   Haydar,
>   amber-scented, smarigdite green.
> Look: it is offered to you by a slender Turk-
>   ish gazelle
>   who sways delicate as a willow bough.
> As he prepares it, you might compare it
>   to the traces of fine down on a blushing
>   cheek
> since even the slightest breeze makes it
>   move
>   as if in the coolness of a drunken morning
> when silvery pigeons might whisper in
>   branches
>   filling its vegetal soul with their mutual
>   emotions.
> How many meanings it has, significances
>   unknown to wine!
>   So close your ears to the Old Censor's
>   slander!

("Haydar", a legendary Khorassanian sufi ascetic, was supposed to have discovered the spiritual uses of hashish.)

One of the companions of Ibn Arabi, an "elegant young poet" from North Africa named Afif Tilimsani, compared the tresses of the Beloved to hashish and the mouth to wine. Once however at a party he was offered hashish by a friend named Juban al-Qawwas, who said,

> When opportunity arises, seize it,
>   since the time for savoring it is brief.
> Take pleasure from something amber-scented,
>   touched with green as myrtle-leaf.

Tilimsani refused the drug and answered:

> They say it expands the consciousness, this
>   grass.
> Why then, the greatest intellect must be the
>   ass!

Other sufis however were prepared to defend hashish
in the highest terms. The Turkish sufi poet Fuzuli (author
of a *Layla and Majnun* which has been translated into
English) wrote a treatise on "Bhang and Wine" in which
he claimed that wine is merely "an eager disciple setting
the world afire", but hashish is the sufi master himself.
Wine shows the way to the hermitage of the Shaykh of
Love—but hashish is the refuge itself. Once a certain sufi
of Basra began to consume hashish regularly; his shaykh
realized this meant he had reached the ultimate degree of
perfection, and no longer stood in need of guidance. This
(says Fuzuli) "proves that hashish is the perfect being,
sought after by mankind with great eagerness. It may not
be the perfect being for everybody, but it most certainly is
for the seeker of mystical experience."

It would be impossible and tedious to recount every
example of spiritual cannabis-use I witnessed, but generally the smoking dervishes I met fell into several categories. A few were con-men and drug salesmen. The majority were amiable lazy wanderers of slight spiritual pretensions,
very much like some of the young Westerners on the road
in the Sixties. One might accuse them of living off the
credulous, of posing as mystics, of social parasitism and
undoubtedly of many infractions of law both civil and
divine. But such characters have a recognized place in
traditional society: the bohemian life of the Qalandar is a
valuable pressure-valve in a world so rigid and formal.

A small but impresive minority of the Qalandars
are—by any fair standards—genuine mystics. For this
assertion I have only my own opinion and no proof.

However, over the years I travelled in the East I met many thousands of people on various spiritual paths and hundreds of gurus, mursheds, fakirs and full-time dervishes. Among the most impressive were several devoted cannabis users. I know that very few orthodox sufis will accept my assertion, since by orthodox definition a drug-user cannot be a true mystic.

But there exist a few exceptions to this blanket condemnation. One extremely well-respected and orthodox Iranian sufi master whom I met, numbered among his disciples an old man who loved to drink wine. When drunk he would recite sufi poetry, weep for joy, sparkle with insights and display all the signs of the *hal* or "spiritual state". The master allowed the old man to drink but forbade his other disciples, saying, "If wine produced in all humans the same state it inspires in our old friend, then the Prophet would never have needed to forbid alchohol!"

In a cemetary in Peshawar I met a cannabis-devoted *maulang* who lived in a packing-case-sized hut amongst the tombs. Physically he reminded me of certain fanatical Hatha-yogis and naked ascetics I met in India, who seem to glow with praeternatural health and happiness. These men (and women) would be noticed even in California, so radiant are they—and in unhealthy India they stand out like beacons. I met another dervish of this type in Herat, and later wrote the following text about my experiences that day:

> "The Prophet used to see the angel Gabriel in the form of Ziya Kalbi, the most beautiful of the youth of Mecca." — hadith

Last time I was in Herat, acting as a guide to a group of film-makers, we had only one full day. We started by driving out of town up toward those bare cliffs on the north side of the highway, overlooking Jami's tomb. At the foot of the cliffs we found the shrine of a saint called Baba Qaltan, "the Rolling Father", who is said to have rolled on the ground instead of walking. Next to the tomb was a large empty courtyard covered with small brown pebbles. The guardian of the shrine explained the ritual to be followed, but of our party I was the only one willing to try. I lay down on my back and rested my head on a broken piece of marble tombstone. The guardian made me fold my arms over my chest and recite some Koranic verses with my eyes closed. He gave me a gentle shove and in order not to disappoint him I rolled a little. Suddenly however I felt the earth tilt on its axis and I rolled, out of control as if down a steep hill. When I rolled to a stop and opened my eyes I was on the far side of the courtyard. I had come to rest facing Mecca, so the guardian told me my faith was pure; if I had faced the other way I would have been a hypocrite. I tipped the guardian and we left.

The film-makers wanted to see the grave of Behzad the Timurid miniaturist. We found it in a cemetary perched on the edge of a cliff with a view of the whole valley. Inside one of the larger mausoleums a group of dervishes were smoking charas and invited us to join them. The film-makers refused, and I myself had not smoked in over a year. Not wishing to seem impolite, I puffed at the pipe in true Afghan style, hyperventilating like a carburetor. We then took our leave, and I noticed immediately that I was as intoxicated as I've ever been in my life: an effect equal to about 500 micrograms of LSD. I could function (in fact my Persian began to improve noticably) but the combination of *baraka* (the spiritual ambience of the tombs) and the Assassin's drug precipitated me into the open, into the crystal-turquoise air, the dun-ochre hills, the vivid pines, the palpability of the world and the invisibility of the spirit. On the way back to the car we met a dervish climbing up. He was dressed in rags and a patched cloak, and his eyes were clear and electric as a hawk's. He addressed me alone of the group, inviting me to return to the tomb with him and smoke more hashish. Attractive as I found him, I could not delay the group, so I declined with many salaams and bows.

Driving back into town we noticed a shrine on the left side of the road, and our Herati driver (who had divined our taste for tombs) pulled over without being asked. It was a typical Afghan mausoleum with the grave on a raised earth platform facing a tiny baked-mudbrick mosque, surrounded by cool trees and fields of herbs. We stood around saying nothing when a boy dressed in turban, shalwar, kurta and vest came up and started speaking to me. About eleven or twelve, handsome with large eyes like the dervish but softer; very bright, very dignified. He told me this was the tomb of Husayn Va'ez Kashefi the translator of the Koran, and that his mother sent him here to pick herbs. (Later I found out that Kashefi also wrote *The Rose Garden of Martyrs,* the first complete book on the deaths of the Shiite Imams—although he himself was a Sunni—and a book on the occult sciences and alchemy. I also learned the story behind his Persian translation of the Koran. It seems that Kashefi was a cataleptic, and fell into a fit, and was taken for dead. They buried him there at that shrine and he woke up later in his coffin. He prayed that if he were released he'd translate the Koran. That night some poor relatives came to dig him up and steal his shroud. He sat up in his grave and I suppose scared them half to death; got up without a word and went home and started to work immediately.)

The boy told me his own name but I didn't get it, so he took my pen and wrote it—very proudly in English letters—on the palm of his hand. Abdul Quddus, Servant of the Holy. Then he asked me to give him my pen, and I did so.

We left (always those film-makers, driving me like a Native Guide!) and motored a bit further down the road and found another shrine—on the right. The driver told us it was Imam Fakhroddin Razi—the polar opposite of

Shaykh Kashefi!—a dry philosopher-theologian and anti-sufi. We fell to photographing the shrine, which was even more beautiful than Kashefi's, totally unchanged since perhaps the fifteenth century—when suddenly a man about forty came up to me and started speaking. He assumed for some reason that I was a Moslem but seemed to suspect me of esoteric tendencies. He became more and more excited and leaned forward till his face was about an inch from mine so I had to keep retreating to avoid the fine spray of spittle. He kept questioning me on points of orthodoxy and I lost track with my bad Persian (and I doubt he was making much sense anyway) till the driver came up and rescued me and told him I was "all right and a true believer and a lover of shrines." So the man apologized and very politely invited us all to lunch, but we politely declined and drove back into town.

❀   ❀   ❀

Although discussing Moslem mystics I cannot resist mentioning the first truly decisive and interesting Hindu saddhu I met in India (in Darjeeling), a rotund and Santa-Claus-bearded man with an impeccable (almost) Oxford accent, named Ganesh Baba, who smoked ganja like no one else I've ever met, like a Rastafarian.* He made a point of knowing and appreciating other paths, including sufism, although his own way was jnana-yoga and tantra. In Bengali tantra, cannabis is sometimes used as a substitute for sacramental wine, according to both Ganesh Baba and also a tantric colleague of his named Sri Kamanaransan Biswas (who initiated me into the worship of Kali). A

---

*The Jamaican word for marijuana is ganja, and presumably reaches the New World from India via Kenya and Ethiopia. The Rastafarians regard cannabis as a sacrament, and the true cult-members ought not to be confused with gangsters operating in North America as "Rastas". The religion has survived the death of its avatar, the emperor Haile Selassie, and Jamaican culture continues to be inspired by Rastafarian symbols and energy. Reggae is only the best-known and most widely exported aspect of Rastafarian art.

small book of Ganesh Baba's paradoxes was published in England once, and recently I came across his face on a postcard sold in New York gift shops, so I presume I was not his only Western acquaintance or devotee. Ganesh Baba was perhaps quite mad (his favorite occupations, aside from smoking ganja, were playing games with children and attacking those adults who failed to show him sufficient respect, his weapon being a tightly-rolled umbrella)—but he was certainly brilliant and sometimes unutterably happy: on the whole, a good advertisement for cannabis use.

In Casteneda's terms, cannabis appears to act as an Ally for certain seekers and not for others. Those who claim to benefit from the herb agree on certain points. Cannabis produces an intoxication which is profound but not overwhelming. Unlike true hallucinogens it does not impair self-control (except in minor and unimportant ways). It permits or facilitates intense concentration, which can be turned toward the Imagination (according to many musicians and other artists, oriental as well as occidental) or toward invocation of the divine Name or other spiritual exercises. It enhances relaxation, amiability, sense perception, intuition, and good cheer: all useful spiritual qualities, one would imagine. Long-term use seems (after centuries of observation dating back to Siberian Neolithic tombsites) to produce no ill effects whatsoever. (Malnutrition can be aggravated by cannabis use, but no evidence exists that the drug in itself causes any deficiency diseases. Chromosomal changes have been observed in users, but only at about the same rate as for coffee and aspirin: apparently meaningless. Positive medical effects are noted by traditional Chinese doctors as well as modern eye-specialists and radiation therapists.)

Cannabis is also the closest thing available in nature to a true aphrodisiac, although no one can say whether this effect is physiological or psychological. Not every smoker experiences the whole spectrum of effects, of

∗ 207 ∗

course. Many, perhaps the majority of users report loss of concentration, uncontrollable fantasy, and an inclination to do nothing much in particular (especially not hard labor!). Those for whom cannabis acts as an Ally however feel that its benefits are unqualified. Like the old dervish and his wine, they use it because it produces in them a spiritual state at once subtle but deep, and lends them an energy needed to transcend the sloth and dullness which envelope the Evanescent World of Illusion, greed, violence and slavery.

To those who argue that a spiritual state acquired by drugs is not a "real state", the users reply that lack of awareness is a sort of disease and ganja is the medicine for it. Would anyone dare claim that someone cured of, say, diabetes by insulin was not "really healthy" because he'd used a drug to defeat his illness?

Cannabis has never, so far as I know, been worshipped as a god in itself (like the Magic Mushroom or wine or peyote or soma). Apparently it is always seen as a potentiator, a tool rather than as an end in itself. In this it performs admirably for Moslems, who are perhaps temperamentally unsuited to drugs so potent as to become "idols" in their own right. Although the ulema class cannabis as an intoxicant, no one who uses it as an Ally ever feels "drunk" on it, or swept out of control as if by mescaline or lysergic acid.

Nevertheless of course the mullas are in a sense correct. Cannabis is intoxicating in a way that the opiates, for example, are not—despite their greater strength and addictiveness. Opium, say the mullas, affects the body, cannabis the mind. In fact some of the Persian Shiite ulema have even declared that opium is not forbidden *(haram)* but only non-recommended *(makru)*. The cynical would point out that a great many Persian mullas are opium addicts. But the fact would still remain: there exists a qualitative difference between cannabis and opium in their effects on the ego (in a very loose sense of that word).

Cannabis was not as widely used in Iran in the 70's as in Afghanistan and India. A Persian preparation called *dugh-i vahdat* was often mentioned but I never sampled any. A literal translation of the term would be "buttermilk of the divine Unity": a mixture of water, yoghurt and hashish.

In the past however hashish must have been much more popular among the Persian heterodox mystics. The question of the Assassins or Hashisheen (a faulty etymology) has been discussed elsewhere; but here we may pause to ask whether cannabis users might not prove to be rather poor killers (it certainly seems true of the modern Egyptian army, for example). It appears unlikely indeed that Assassin *fedayeen* were ever sent forth on their work intoxicated. Indeed, Marco Polo claims that the Assassin drug (hashish mixed with opium, one would guess) was used to trick the recruits into believing themselves in Paradise, when in truth they had simply been spirited into the lush gardens of Alamut, or of the even larger stronghold in Syria. Even if this tale be dismissed as nonsense one might still insist that so much smoke must indicate some smoke. If the medieval Assassins used cannabis (and they certainly drank wine) it seems logical to assume that they did so largely as today's Qalandars do, as an aid to meditation and as a pleasure allowed to the initiate, even if forbidden to the profane.

The Persian word for opium is *teriak,* from the Greek *theriac,* Universal Medicine or Cure-all. It is usually smoked in a milder form in Iran than the *chendoh* or *shireh* popular farther East. The raw opium is cleaned but not boiled down or strengthened with morphine-base pipe-ash. The Iranian pipe *(bafur)* is also less efficient than the Chinese-style *chendoh* pipe. Persian addicts often like to fraternize while they smoke, usually at home rather than in a den. An occasional pipe or even a slight habit is not considered a very scandalous matter even in quite upper-class and traditional circles. A mature gentleman—be he courtier, mulla, sufi, profesor, merchant or whatever—may like to share the brazier *(mangal)* with a few cronies, drink tea, listen to classical Persian music, discuss poetry and philosophy: all very traditional and discreet, and a far cry from the louche image of the oriental junky.

One of Iran's leading turbanned theologians, an expert in mystical Shiite philosophy, a man so respected that neither the Shah nor Khomeini has dared order him silent (he averages three or four books a year), is a well-known opium addict. So are a great many sufis, especially in Kerman province, but also in every province and city of Iran. So are many artists, musicians, writers and aristocrats as well as peasants and laborers. Opium smoking is "socialized" in traditional Iran to a much greater degree than any other place I know.

I have heard some sufis claim spiritual benefits from opium, usually on the grounds that by releasing them from tension and sadness it allows them to concentrate on spiritual matters. One can detect a whiff of opium in much Persian art, a kind of dreamy un-centered serenity tinged with melancholy and a drifting toward sleep. This opiated flavor in Iranian culture certainly fails to represent the Persian genius at its most vivid and acute. Nevertheless it would be churlish to deny all spiritual value to such a decorative quietism, or to the drug which sometimes inspires it. Addiction is viewed as a crime in our society, and it may be difficult for us to associate opium and mysticism. Other societies have different preconceptions, and we need not share them in order to understand them.

Cannabis in the form of kif is widely used in North Africa. Egypt and Syria consume Lebanese hashish, some of it equal in quality to the best Afghan—particularly the red and gold from Baalbek province, largely raised and sold by Shiite tribesmen. Turkey produces an excellent "grey" hashish, and the very word "opium" is of course Turkish (after the town of Afyon). Both sufism and cannabis use are reported from the island of Sumatra, and from East Africa. Dervishes of Pakistan are said to migrate in the summer to the province of Kafiristan, "Land of the Infidels", which straddles the Pak-Afghan border. The Afghan Kafirs, called Nuristanis, have been converted to Islam—only a few decades ago—but on the Pakistani side of the valley a pagan religion is still practised (presumably a survival of the original Aryan invasion). Superior hashish is produced here, and the Kafir women are rumored more hospitable than Moslem ladies in purdah. Suggestive examples linking syncretistic mysticism and cannabis or other drug use could be multiplied, even in the Islamic world, without mentioning other religions and cultures.

But such information can be found readily in books. I have concentrated on personal experience in this Chapter because in such a nebulous and little-studied field even subjective accounts and intuitions may help lead toward clarity. No one would question the fact that some Moslems use cannabis. Seldom however has anyone asked why? or how?

The best answer to these questions would avoid all sociologizing and psychologizing, and attempt to express the point of view of a heterodox Moslem mystic in a language appropriate to the phenomenon under study: his life and beliefs. The following account cannot claim authenticity—since it is an imaginative construct rather than an actual statement by that hypothetical Moslem— but perhaps it might be considered fair and reasonably representational.

Humankind in its "ordinary" state lacks the attentiveness and will to recognize the Real. We need help. And since the Real itself is "generous", constantly revealing itself to "those with eyes to see," such help can come from many sources.

Intoxication provides one major source of aid in breaking out of the shell of our stale illusions. Sufis have argued ad nauseum whether Sobriety is better than Intoxication. Among those who supported spiritual drunkenness perhaps the most famous was Mansur al-Hallaj, who was executed for heresy.

But God himself approves of intoxication, since he promises it to the inhabitants of paradise in innumerable Koranic passages. However, "he who tastes the wine of this world will not taste that of Paradise" (hadith). Material wine is forbidden, only spiritual wine permitted. Many sufi poets never drank a drop, for all their mystic wine-songs. To paraphrase Rumi, if grape-wine could make one into a mystic, then every sot in the gutter would be a saint. The mystic lends his intoxication to wine, not the wine to the mystic. This is the orthodox mystical view.

"Do not approach prayer while intoxicated." This hadith is given a radical exegesis by some sufis. They take it to mean that intoxication is better than prayer and that the esotericist is absolved from ritual duty by his spiritual state. As the Ismailis would say, those who have tasted the kernel can discard the shell. Those who adopt this attitude may still consider themselves Moslems, but have decidedly stepped outside the Shariah.

For such a heretic the sources of intoxication lose all moral stigma. A vagrant breeze, a beautiful face, a watered garden, a pitcher of wine or a pipe of hashish—these all become prayer in themselves, or better than prayer. For supplication need be made only by those who have not entered. For those who see here-and-now with the eyes of paradise, nothing which sharpens that vision can be considered forbidden.

However, actual wine, while enjoyable and even spiritually refreshing in moderation, seems only rarely to produce in humans of this Age the true dionysan ecstasis. (Ethnomycologists think Bacchus may have laced the Maenads' cup with *amanita*.) But cannabis inspires some of its devotees with precisely the sort of "state" which the Koran appears to associate with paradisal wine, which "causes no headaches", and enhances the play of love with houris and cup-boys. Cannabis is green, the color of Islam, and the color of the Hidden Prophet of sufism, Khezr the Green Man, the immortal ruler of Hyperborea, Alexander's cook, servant of Moses, discoverer of the Fountain of Youth, initiator of sufis who have no human master, a vegetation spirit in whose footsteps flowers and herbs sprout by magic. Green is the highest color in certain systems of sufi alchemy.

Moreover, although the ulema concur in banning it, the Koran itself makes no mention of cannabis, nor do the hadith (at least not in any collection known to me). If the ulema of Istanbul could use such an argument to allow Hanafis to drink beer, it might well be used by sufis mystics to justify bhang. The true "heretic" will reject such legal loop-holery, as will the truly orthodox. But ordinary Moslems have been known to argue in this fashion.

Finally the only true apologia must be made on the basis of self-knowledge. Anything—even including religion—can act as a poison against perception, or as a support for contemplation of the Real. As the Koran itself says, "Which of your Lôrd's bounties would you deny?" The Green Parrot takes some travellers to paradise, and for them Faith and Infidelity are equally meaningless.

Descriptive Bibliography:
A Guide to Further Reading

This is by no means a definitive bibliography on Islamic heresy in general or indeed on any of the topics discussed in *Scandal*. Most of the works mentioned here are major and seminal studies, and many contain bibliographies of other works (which in turn will contain further bibliographies and so on ad infinitum till the mind collapses under the weight of a million dusty tomes).

Whenever a source in English exists I have listed it in preference to works in other languages. Some French and German titles are listed because they are the only books about the subjects they discuss. Again, I have included no articles from learned journals unless I actually used them myself, or unless they are the only source for a given subject.

The *Encyclopaedia of Islam* and the *Shorter Encyclopaedia of Islam* contain articles on many of the topics in *Scandal,* some of them inadequate and others brilliant; and all with yet more bibliographical clues to follow.

Abdel Kader, Ali Hassan, *The Life, Personality and Writings of al-Junayd* (London, 1962). (Hallaj's *murshed,* the keystone of orthodox sufism—unfortunately the book is competent but not fascinating.)

Algar, Hamid, *Religion and State in Iran, 1758-1906: The Role of the 'Ulama in the Qajar Period* (Los Angeles, 1969). (A lucid and highly readable study, a key to understanding Iranian history from the fall of the Safavids to yesterday's newspaper.)

Algar, Hamid, "The Revolt of the Agha Khan Mahallati and the Transference of the Isma'ili Imamate to India", in *Studia Islamica* (ex fasc. XXIX, 1969).

Arberry, A.J., *Classical Persian Literature* (London, 1958). (More up-to-date but less engaging than Browne's *Literary History,* q.v.)

Arberry, A.J., (trans.), *The Koran Interpreted* (London, 1964). (The most poetic Englishing of the Koran, and Arberry's most inspired work.)

Bell, J.N., *Love Theory in Later Hanbalite Islam* (Albany, 1979). (A dense and scholarly study with a great deal of information on *shahed-bazi,* especially as viewed by its most bigoted enemies, such as Ibn Taymiyya.)

Birge, J., *The Bektashi Order of Dervishes* (London, 1965). (A sound monograph on a heretical Turkish sufi order.)

Browne, E.G., *A Literary History of Persia* (four volumes;

Cambridge, 1956). (Browne had a prejudice in favor of heresies, and exemplary taste in Persian literature. A most enjoyable reference work.)

Chadwick, Nora, *Poetry and Prophecy* (Cambridge, 1942). (A wonderful book full of "poetic facts" by an expert on epic literature; a study of the bard as *vates,* shaman-poet and seer.)

Corbin, Henry, *Creative Imagination in the Sufism of Ibn 'Arabi,* trans. R. Manheim (Princeton, 1969). (An essential book for the understanding of Ibn Arabi and the best introduction to the vital and difficult work of Corbin, all of whose writings are important sources for the present work.)

Corbin, H., *The Man of Light in Iranian Sufism,* trans. N. Pearson (Boulder, Colo., 1978).

Corbin, H., *Spiritual Body and Celestial Earth: From Mazdean to Shi'ite Iran,* trans. N. Pearson (Princeton, 1977).

Dara Shikoh, *Majma'-ul-Bahrain, or, The Mingling of the Two Oceans,* trans. M. Mahfuz-ul-Haq (Calcutta, 1929). ("The vedanta of the Hindus is the same as our sufism." The classic source of Hindu-Moslem rapprochement and syncretism, by a Moghul prince.)

Geertz, Clifford, *The Religion of Java* (Glencoe, Ill., 1960). (The essential book on Javanese syncretism by an intelligent anthropologist-sociologist.)

Guénon, René, *The Reign of Quantity and the Signs of the Times,* trans. Lord Northbourne (London, 1953). (Guénon's best book, brilliant, gloomy and irrascible; the classic text on the idea of Tradition which has influenced writers like S.H. Nasr, F. Schuon, T. Burckhardt and the circle who publish in *Studies in Comparative Religion*. Guénon converted to Islam; as defenders of orthodoxy, he and his followers are most severe toward "heresy" and go to great lengths to reconcile the Law and the Path.)

Hafez, Shamsoddin Muhammad, *The Divan,* trans. H. Wilberforce Clarke (two volumes; London, 1974).

Hafez, S.M., *Teachings of Hafez (Divan),* trans. Gertrude Bell (London, 1979). (Hafez is perhaps impossible to translate. The Wilberforce Clarke versions are by an eccentric British soldier who seems to have been initiated into sufism; the Bell versions are decent poetic attempts by a famous lady spy; and both books are more-or-less in print. A great many other people have tried, including a team composed of Peter Avery and John Heath-Stubbs. The more translations of Hafez one reads, the better.)

Hallaj, Husayn ibn Mansur, *Le Diwan d'al-Hallaj,* ed. et trad. par Louis Massignon (Paris, 1955). (Unfortunately not yet translated into English.)

Hallaj, H., *The Tawasin of Mansur al-Hallaj,* trans. A. Abd ar-Rahman at-Tarjumana (Berkeley, 1974). (An excellent translation with an utterly useless introduction and commentary. This is Hallaj's apologia for Satan.)

Hodgson, Marshall G.S., *The Order of Assassins* (New York, 1980). (The only book any non-scholar needs to read on Ismaili history; lucid, entertaining and sympathetic.)

Hollister, John N., *The Shi'a of India* (London, 1953). (Outdated and missionary-oriented, but still informative.)

Ibn Arabi, Muhyiddin, *The Bezels of Wisdom (Fusus al-*

hikam), trans. R.W.J. Austin (New York, 1980). (A complete translation, superceding all earlier partial and less-scholarly renditions. Ibn Arabi's most important work, at least among those available in English.)

Ibn Arabi, M., *Sufis of Andalusia,* trans. R.W.J. Austin (London, 1971). (The Greatest Shaykh's own account of his travels and meetings with fellow sufis—and the Hidden Prophet, Khezr.)

Ibn Arabi, M., *The Tarjuman al-Ashwaq: A Collection of Mystical Odes by Muhyi'ddin ibn al-'Arabi,* trans. R.A. Nicholson (London, 1978). (The Victorian versions of the poems are difficult to read. Ibn Arabi's own commentary is only partially translated. This book deserves a new and complete translation.)

Ibn Arabi, M., et. al., *Journal of the Muhyiddin Ibn 'Arabi Society* (34 East Street, Fritwell, near Bicester, Oxon., England). (A new journal—the first number contains a translation of Ibn Arabi's own summary of the *Fusus al-hikam.*)

Iraqi, Fakhroddin, *Divine Flashes (The Lama'at),* trans. and introductions by William C. Chittick and Peter Lamborn Wilson (New York, 1982). (The "School of Love" according to the "School of Ibn Arabi", couched in a mixture of poetry and poetic prose; Iraqi's masterpiece. For this version, published by a Catholic press, I was obliged to remove all references to boy-love from the biographical introduction. I have made use of the excised material in *Scandal.)*

Iraqi, F., *Kulliyat,* ed. S. Nafisi (Tehran, 1338 AHS/1959). (The Persian source for Iraqi's biography and the "Wine Songs".)

Iraqi, F., *The Song of Lovers (Ushshaq-nama)*, trans. A.J. Arberry (London, 1939). (A partial biography of Iraqi and a terrible translation of one of his long poems.)

Ivanov, Vladimir A., *Alamut and Lamasar, Two Medieval Ismaili Strongholds* (Tehran, 1960). (Ivanov was an eccentric White Russian scholar of Persian and Indian heresies, especially Ismailism. His work is sometimes almost a parody of the scholarly style, but occasionally fascinating. This is one of his best works, informative, scientific and passionately pro-Ismaili.)

Ivanov, V.A., *The Truth-worshippers of Kurdistan; Ahl-i Haqq Texts* (Leiden, 1953). (A farrago of fragments and misinformation but the only book in English on the subject. See, however, the excellent article in the *Encyclopaedia of Islam* by V. Minorski, another Russian.)

Izutsu, Toshihiko, *Sufism and Taoism* (London, 1984). (A revised edition of his hard-to-find *Comparative Study of the Key Philosophical Concepts in Sufism and Taoism— Ibn Arabi and Lao Tzu, Chuang Tzu;* the best general work on Ibn Arabi in English, and also a brilliant exercise in comparative religion.)

Kermani, Awhadoddin, *Heart's Witness: The Sufi Quatrains of Awhadoddin Kermani,* trans. and introductions by Bernd Manuel Weischer and Peter Lamborn Wilson (Tehran, 1978). (Contains a life of Kermani, and the Persian texts, with English translations, of all his known quatrains except for the ten in Chapter Four of *Scandal*, which were discovered by Prof. Weischer after *Heart's Witness* had already been published.)

Khusraw, Nasir, *Nasir-e Khusraw: Forty Poems from the Divan,* trans. and introductions by G.-R. Aavani and Peter Lamborn Wilson (Tehran, 1977). (Poems by the famous traveller and Ismaili missionary of the pre-Alamut period.)

Lincoln, Charles Eric, *The Black Muslims in America* (Boston, 1973). (Information on Noble Drew Ali and the Moorish Science Temple.)

Massignon, Louis, *La Passion de Husayn Ibn Mansur Hallaj* (Paris, 1975). (Sadly still untranslated into English; contains the hagiographical biography of the martyr-sufi.)

Nasr, Seyyed Hossein, *Three Muslim Sages (Avicenna, Sohrawardi, Ibn Arabi)* (Cambridge, Mass., 1964). (An engaging and informative work—and still the only good introduction to Sohrawardi in English.)

Pope, Arthur Upham (ed.), *A Survey of Persian Art* (fifteen volumes, incl. indices and addenda; London, 1939). (The magnum opus on Persian art—everything one needs to know about the classical tradition, and some information on popular art as well.)

Pourjavady, Nasrollah, and Peter Lamborn Wilson, "Isma'ilis and Ni'matullahis", in *Studia Islamica* XLI, 1975.

Pourjavady, N., and Peter Lamborn Wilson, *Kings of Love: The History and Poetry of the Ni'matullahi Sufi Order of Iran* (Tehran, 1978).

Ramanujan, A.K. (trans), *Speaking of Siva* (Middlesex, 1963). (Delightfully good and contemporary translations of the songs of the Lingayat saddhus or "Phallus Worshippers".)

Ritter, Hellmut, *Das Meer des Seele: Mensch, Welt und*

Gott in den Geschichten des Fariduddin 'Attar (Leiden, 1955). ("The Sea of Soul"—contains much information on *shahed-bazi* in the context of a study of Attar, whose *Conference of the Birds* is an essential sufi text. Ritter's magnum opus ought to be translated into English.)

Robson, James (ed. and trans.), *Tracts on Listening to Music* (London, 1938). (This book contains the *Bawariq al-ilma* by Ahmad Ghazzali. Not only does this essay comprise the ultimate defense of sufi music, it is also the only work in English by this major sufi figure—until my friend Nasrollah Pourjavady publishes his translation of Ghazzali's great *Sawaneh,* promised by Routledge and Kegan Paul.)

Rosenthal, Franz, *The Herb: Hashish versus Medieval Muslim Society* (Leiden, 1971). (The only solid scholarship on the subject of hashish in Islam, but somewhat staid and serious. I've taken the liberty of trying to enliven some of his translations of hashish poems.)

Rumi, Jalaloddin, *The Mathnawi of Jalal al-Din Rumi,* trans. and commentaries by R.A. Nicholson (London, 1960). (The ocean of sufism, perhaps the greatest work of Persian literature, the ultimate textbook of Islamic esotericism, "The Koran in Persian"; a scholarly literal translation with the risqué stories done into Latin!)

Rypka, Jan, *History of Iranian Literature* (Dordrecht, 1968). (Written with a marxist slant, and so occasionally useful—if tendentious—when dealing with heretics.)

Savory, Roger, *Iran Under The Safavids* (Cambridge/ New York, 1980). (A sound attempt to make sense of the bewildering story of the Safavid "theocracy".)

Schlamminger, Karl, and Peter Lamborn Wilson, *Persische*

Bildteppiche: Genupfte Mythen. Weaver of Tales: Persian Picture Rugs, preface by Basil W. Robinson (Munich, 1980). (The text is in German and English, but I have felt free to quote at length since the book has never been marketed in the English-speaking world, and besides that it costs nearly seventy dollars!)

Schroeder, Eric, *Muhammad's People: a tale by anthology. The religion and politics, poetry and violence, science, ribaldry and finance of the Muslims, from the age of ignorance before Islam and the mission of God's prophet to sophistication in the eleventh century; a mosaic translation.* (Portland, Maine; the Bond Wheelwright Co.; 1955). (This hard-to-find text can be ordered from the publisher. It is an indispensable introduction to Islamic culture, an entire education in one superb book.)

Shabestari, Mahmud, *Gulshan-i raz, The Mystic Rose Garden,* trans. E.H. Whinfield (London, 1880). (This inadequate translation will eventually be superceded by S.H. Nasr, who will publish a new version with the Paulist Press in New York. Shabestari wrote only this one amazing work, as a very young man. It contains the whole of sufism—or at least the sufism of the Persian followers of Ibn Arabi—in slightly over a thousand lines.)

Subhan, John A., *Sufism: Its Saints and Shrines* (Lucknow, 1960). (Another book by a missionary—but still the only source in English for some of the wilder manifestations of Indian sufism.)

Surieu, Robert, *Sarv e Naz* (Geneva, 1967). (Persian erotic miniatures, including a number with pederastic themes; and some information on *shahed-bazi*.)

Trimmingham, J. Spencer, *The Sufi Orders In Islam*

(Oxford, 1971). (Solid information as far as it goes; useful and accurate only for certain areas.)

Tusi, Nasiroddin Muhammad, *Rawdatu'l-Taslim, commonly called Tasawwurat,* trans. V.A. Ivanov (Leiden, 1950). (Tusi was a "Twelver" Shiite, not an Ismaili. He was hired to write on Ismailism by the hierarchs of Alamut, but after the sect was nearly destroyed by the Mongols, Tusi hired out to them instead, like a true professional scientist of our own days.)

Valiuddin, Mir, *Love of God, the Sufi Approach* (Hyderabad, India, 1968). (A great deal of information on love theory and *shahed-bazi,* presented in a charming and totally disorganized way by an Indian sufi.)

Wilson, Peter Lamborn, *Angels* (London/New York, 1980). (Some information on the relation between love theory and angelology; a popularization of Corbin, with lots of pictures.)

Yazdani, G., *Bidar, its History and Monuments* (Oxford, 1947). (Information on the Nematollahi Order in India.)